T0320157

Teaching the History of Economic Thought

ELGAR GUIDES TO TEACHING

The Elgar Guides to Teaching series provides a variety of resources for instructors looking for new ways to engage students. Each volume provides a unique set of materials and insights that will help both new and seasoned teachers expand their toolbox in order to teach more effectively. Titles include selections of methods, exercises, games and teaching philosophies suitable for the particular subject featured. Each volume is authored or edited by a seasoned professor. Edited volumes comprise contributions from both established instructors and newer faculty who offer fresh takes on their fields of study.

Titles in the series include:

Classroom Exercises for Entrepreneurship
A Cross-Disciplinary Approach
James D. Hart

Teaching the History of Economic Thought
Integrating Historical Perspectives into Modern Economics
Edited by Daniela Tavasci and Luigi Ventimiglia

Teaching the History of Economic Thought

Integrating Historical Perspectives into Modern Economics

Edited by

Daniela Tavasci

School of Economics and Finance, Queen Mary University of London, UK

Luigi Ventimiglia

School of Economics and Finance, Queen Mary University of London, UK

ELGAR GUIDES TO TEACHING

Cheltenham, UK • Northampton, MA, USA

Published by
Edward Elgar Publishing Limited
The Lypiatts
15 Lansdown Road
Cheltenham
Glos GL50 2JA
UK

Edward Elgar Publishing, Inc.
William Pratt House
9 Dewey Court
Northampton
Massachusetts 01060
USA

A catalogue record for this book
is available from the British Library

Library of Congress Control Number: 2017959994

This book is available electronically in the **Elgar**online
Economics subject collection
DOI 10.4337/9781788113489

MIX
Paper from
responsible sources
FSC   FSC® C013056
www.fsc.org

ISBN 978 1 78811 347 2 (cased)
ISBN 978 1 78811 348 9 (eBook)

Typeset by Servis Filmsetting Ltd, Stockport, Cheshire
Printed and bound in Great Britain by TJ International Ltd, Padstow

Contents

Contributors

Riccardo Bellofiore, Professor, University of Bergamo, Italy

Gerald Friedman, Professor, University of Massachusetts at Amherst, USA

Stephanie Fuller, Education Adviser, Queen Mary University of London, UK

Joseph Halevi, Honorary Staff Member, University of Sydney, Australia, and Professor at the International University College of Turin, Italy

Constantinos Repapis, Lecturer, Goldsmiths, University of London, UK

Louis-Philippe Rochon, Full Professor, Laurentian University, Canada

Sergio Rossi, Full Professor, University of Fribourg, Switzerland

Daniela Tavasci, Senior Lecturer, Queen Mary University of London, UK

Luigi Ventimiglia, Lecturer, Queen Mary University of London, UK

1. Introduction

Daniela Tavasci and Luigi Ventimiglia

The idea of this volume stemmed from our teaching experience at the School of Economics and Finance at Queen Mary University of London (QMUL). When Daniela first joined the department, she was asked to launch a module on the history of economic thought (HET) for second- and third-year undergraduate students. In the wake of the financial crisis, students had been exposed to numerous commentaries and articles in the specialist media, which had referred to Marx, Minsky, and a number of other past economists they had never heard of. They were interested in reading about these economists and so they asked the head of the department to include HET in the curriculum.

When Luigi joined the department, he was asked to make substantial changes to a finance module taught at Master's level. He thought one way to do this successfully was to channel his professional background as a fund manager and his heterodox experience gained at the School of Oriental and African Studies into the redesign of the module. The module received outstanding teaching evaluations and, as a result, Luigi was asked to do the same for a similar undergraduate module.

Both Daniela and Luigi decided to introduce a new approach that was student centred, that historically contextualized economic and financial theories and models, that was able to introduce pluralism, and that was inspired by problem-based learning (PBL). Over the years, by evaluating and further reflecting on this teaching approach, we decided to call it 'teaching with historical perspectives' (THP). Our adaptation of the standard PBL into THP is based on the idea that students are presented with the same problems that economists of the past had faced, and so it is possible for students to *retrace* the interpretations, solutions and policy prescriptions that these past economists had provided for their problems. Each economic theory

1

then is not just a model taken from the textbook, it is a solution that one specific economist produced in response to a specific real economic problem or, increasingly frequently in more recent times, as a result of debates within the discipline.

Nevertheless, a specific solution to an actual economic problem is rarely the only one. Thus, THP presents various historical perspectives to the same problem and exposes students to both the evolution of economic reality and the corresponding evolution of the history of economic thought, as a result of both changes in the actual economy and debates amongst various economists and schools of thought. In other words, this approach allows the lecturer to move beyond the static categorizations of standard textbooks and provides a pluralistic approach to teaching that is historically framed with respect both to the historical contextualization of the phenomena under investigation *and* to how various systems of economic thought have looked at those phenomena and sets of variables throughout history. In this respect then, THP provides a context and an experience of teaching and learning with authenticity and pluralism. As a result, it not only engages students in the classroom, it also helps them to develop the problem-solving and debating skills that are so essential for a professional economist.

With respect to the design and planning of THP in the classroom, we started to test this approach at the School of Economics and Finance at QMUL in 2013, in the teaching of the HET module for levels 5 and 6 and the finance modules for levels 5, 6 and 7. The aims of introducing THP were to improve teaching evaluation, enhance students' engagement with the subject, improve problem-solving capacity, foster students' social links, and facilitate the development of transferrable skills in the context of economics and finance. We also wanted to improve students' engagement in the context of very diverse backgrounds and educational needs. Finally, and most importantly, the approach would improve the mechanisms for feedback and increase its frequency, since academics and students would be in a position of enhanced social interaction, facilitating feedback in both directions. This more continuous dialogue would result in a more reflective approach to teaching and learning.

The approach is made clear to students mainly in terms of the structure of the module: for example, the evolution of financial theory from the capital asset pricing model (CAPM) to the arbitrage pricing theory (APT) is historically contextualized to enable students to discuss the evolution of financial theory. As a result, these two theories are no longer seen as disconnected; instead, they are looked at in relation to one another. Similarly, in the HET module, various schools of thought are introduced following a chronological sequence. However, these are not seen as exhibiting a linear development. Rather, various systems of thought are analysed as competing theories, and the (sometimes fierce) debates between economists are discussed. An important example is the debate between Keynes and Hayek. In this respect then, the modules are designed along two dimensions: a vertical dimension, which just follows the standard chronological order that is often adopted by textbooks, and a horizontal dimension, which follows specific topics and questions along the vertical dimension. An example of the horizontal dimension from the HET module is questions related to value or to price determination. An example from the finance module is how the efficiency of financial markets has been tackled using various methods, given the link between the horizontal dimension and different interpretations of uncertainty and risk. These are fundamental questions that are neglected in standard textbooks and addressed only as peripheral assumptions or ignored completely. Topics such as these tend to question the approach generally used in standard textbooks, since THP considers various perspectives that compete with the mainstream.

The introduction of THP made us nervous at first. Students were asked to do more work: as well as studying their textbooks and answering standard questions or applying formulae to solve finance exercises, they were asked to read original journal articles or extracts from books written hundreds of years ago. Nevertheless, evaluations of the new approach were very encouraging: students were engaging with and appreciating this new method because it gave sense and structure to the entire module. Theories and models were no longer coming from nowhere, but had specific origins. Moreover, a problem could be approached from various angles, each emphasizing a distinctive aspect. For a minority of students, especially those studying the finance module, the concern was that this effort was made at the expense of acquiring the technical apparatus that is considered so essential in terms of employability. Some adjustments therefore had to be made to show that THP provides critical thinking skills that are just as necessary. The recent financial crisis helped in this respect, since a number of economists who worked in financial institutions

had published articles in the *Financial Times* discussing past economists and comparing the recent crisis with previous ones.

We also decided to seek more student evaluation by setting up
questionnaires for the last two cohorts of students. These will be
shown in more detail in our individual chapters (Chapters 4 and
8). However, they confirmed that both modules were essential in
exposing students to pluralism in economics and finance and that
the historical perspective gave a helpful overarching structure. In
addition, students commented that the historical perspective in
conjunction with the problem-based approach also helped them put
other modules into perspective.

Having experimented and evaluated this approach, we decided to
host a one-day meeting at QMUL and invited a number of heterodox
economists and teachers of HET from various UK and European
universities. The Learning and Teaching Institute of QMUL was also
involved. The meeting was successful in at least two respects: first,
it was welcomed with enthusiasm and had wide participation, with
40 people attending; second, it allowed us to further reflect on the
approach and refine it in a number of ways.

First, we realized that our approach was innovative, primarily because, unlike traditional HET modules, THP proposes an
integration of the historical perspective into other modules. A
further strength derives from THP as student-centred, interactive
and inspired by a problem-based approach, allowing the lecturers to
manage this integration in a way that is tailored not only to the skills
and knowledge of their students, but also to the specific subject or
subdiscipline being taught.

Second, nevertheless, it is important to clarify what THP is *not*
about. One of the participants to the meeting highlighted how THP
represented a limited historical contextualization. As a result, we
were forced to think very deeply about this critique and, to our surprise, it was a QMUL colleague from the medical school who came
to the rescue. She shared with us the experience of a similar debate
within her own discipline: for medical science, controversy about
whether and how to teach the history of the discipline is now several
decades old: the two opposing camps represent, respectively, those
who support a historical contextualization in teaching the discipline,
and the historians of the discipline who are 'purist' and believe that
history is a serious matter that cannot be reduced merely to the introduction of a timeline. THP does not propose replacing economic

history or the practice and research of the history of economic thought. All THP can do, with existing modules, is to integrate a historical contextualization into them. This contextualization refers to notions, definition, concepts and problems that are discussed in the classroom with respect to both the historical contexts in which they arose in the first place – later being adapted and transformed over the years – and the history of a discipline. It also considers that the history of a discipline has evolved within economics, this was not only in relation and in response to actual economic problems, but also as a result of debates and controversies.

The book is divided into two parts: the first five chapters focus directly on the history of economic thought, the remaining chapters look at examples of how the history of economic thought could be integrated into teaching economics and its various subdisciplines. A number of topics recur throughout the volume.

First, THP shares with the authors of these chapters the idea that economics has not evolved into a perfect discipline. Also, it does not benefit students to be led to believe that theories alternative to the mainstream are not worth investigation because they fall into the category of the wrong doctrine. On the contrary, exposure to alternative or heterodox theories can benefit students in a number of ways: this is the main reason why a historical contextualization of the discipline is necessary. Current mainstream economics should not be seen as a newer and better version of an older economics. Often students do not realize that mainstream economics is just *current* mainstream economics. Once the concept has been established that mainstream economics did not come from nowhere and is likely to be replaced by another mainstream economics, we have already provided a historical contextualization. In other words, current mainstream economics is not a better version of an older economics that a more sophisticated mathematical apparatus has allowed us to pursue. Rather, it is an economics that coexists with other schools of thought, each of which has a historical origin and context.

Second, and this is germane to the previous point, this volume is a call for pluralism in economics. A discussion about the controversial definition of pluralism in economics is beyond the scope of this introduction. Nevertheless, it is worth stating that Groenewegen's definition of pluralism as, 'a combination of mainstream economics with more heterodox approaches in such a way that the student is not confused, but better understands the possibilities and limitations of different schools of thought in economics' (Groenewegen, 2007, p. 14), is not what we aim for. THP aims to locate the approaches within various schools and to see them as *systems* of thought generated within particular historical and intellectual contexts. The historical approach to the teaching of economics, based on both the teaching of economics in history and on its application to real-world problems, has the immediate consequence of helping students to put mainstream economics into perspective and, more specifically, into a *historical* perspective. The THP approach involves a reflection on the notion that methods of enquiry and methodologies identify features of a system of thought. This necessarily requires that even the econometric technical apparatus of current mainstream economics, which is assigned so much importance in the evolution of the discipline and its teaching today, must be put into perspective. Students are also invited to discuss the fact that, after all, many ground-breaking articles have been written without including so much as a single equation.[1] Nevertheless, for this approach to work effectively, it is essential to see pluralism as entailing different, competing views and to recognize that economics 'contains more than one approach, more than one theory and more than one proposed solution to every problem it faces' (Freeman, 2007, p. 7). But what do we mean for this approach to work effectively? The aims of the THP approach are manifold: the first is to satisfy the intellectual requirement that economics students should *discuss* economic issues rather than being presented with the pretence that economics has evolved into a monolithic system with the objectivity of a physical science, which the mathematics of its technical apparatus has increasingly encouraged. *Discuss* means being able to see various aspects of a question. In this respect then, the second aim is to foster and encourage critical thinking. Pluralism and critical thinking are closely interrelated: the THP approach thus embraces the idea that a definition of pluralism involves the fostering of critical thinking and intellectual autonomy (Garnett, 2009).

The third aim, which is a consequence of the previous points, is to engage students. This is viable when students see both the historical contextualization of specific theories and models and the applicability to past and current real-life events and arguments. Finally, with the historical context, it is often easier for economists to bring the social dimension of other schools of thought back into economics.

The first shared experience of this volume is presented in Chapter

2 by Constantinos Repapis. This is an example of how HET might be integrated into undergraduate curricula very effectively in order to tackle the problems of a discipline that tends to forget its own history. The chapter suggests that HET becomes a first-year module equipping students with a contextualization from the beginning as opposed to a trace-back ex post. A first-year HET module would provide an overarching framework for current issues and problematizations and would play a much more integrated role in other modules.

Chapter 3, by Joseph Halevi, is an account of his own personal experience of teaching and learning HET. He touches on a number of issues that have inspired THP with respect to the evolution of economics as a discipline and to pluralism in economics. HET helps to clarify the fact that economics has not evolved linearly and that the current general equilibrium-based economics is not the result of successive improvements in the discipline. Rather, it coexists with other schools of thought. Halevi refers to Sraffa in a passage that is used in both of our modules to explain to students the coexistence of concurrent ways of looking at the same economic reality. Sraffa wrote that the old classical economists had depicted 'the original picture of the system of production and consumption as a circular process and it stands in striking contrast to the view presented by modern theory, of a one-way avenue that leads from "Factors of production" to "Consumption goods"' (Sraffa, 1960, p. 93). In other words, neoclassical economics is not an improved version of classical economics; they coexist and have 'striking[ly]' different views of the economy. This chapter also shows how HET helps students in contextualizing various theories, which is the inspiration for using THP as an adaptation of problem-based learning.

Chapter 4 is by Daniela Tavasci, one of the co-editors of this volume. It addresses a specific example of THP in a History of Economic Thought module and discusses some of the practical aspects of THP.

Chapter 5 is by Riccardo Bellofiore and discusses the experience of an entire tradition, namely the Italian tradition in political economy, within a broader international intellectual context. This chapter contributes to the reflection on how economics has evolved with respect to economic history and its own history as a discipline. This chapter closes the first part of the volume.

The second part of the volume presents examples of experiences of teaching in various subdisciplines. Chapter 6 is authored by

Gerald Friedman and reflects on his experience of teaching a micro-economics module. Interestingly, he considers that the introduction of a historical perspective into his module might help him introduce the foundations of some basic conceptualizations within economics – for example, the social constitution of the demand function as opposed to the assumed specific demand of mainstream economics. This, together with an examination of controversies within economics, engages students. In other words, exposing students to economic debates helps them to engage more directly with the discipline; it is an effective pedagogical tool.

Chapter 7 is co-authored by Louis-Philippe Rochon and Sergio Rossi, who reflect on mainstream economics teaching in general, which affects, in particular, the general conceptualization of money and banking, and these in turn inform policy prescriptions and regulatory frameworks. They also introduce an interesting reflection on methods of enquiry in economics that do not need to be based on econometric techniques. Logic and conceptual rigour can be as effective, if not more so, than econometric techniques and perhaps, in some specific aspects, more appropriate in explaining the nature of money and banking.

Chapter 8 is by the second co-editor of this volume, Luigi Ventimiglia, who is also the co-founder of THP. This chapter presents a discussion around the introduction of THP into a finance module in practice and a reflection on the evaluation of his teaching with this approach.

Chapter 9, the final chapter, presents some avenues for further research. Stephanie Fuller reflects on teaching with historical perspectives in broader terms, beyond economics and its subdisciplines, and provides examples of other disciplines.

We have had discussions with teachers of other disciplines, including the hard sciences, and have seen a number of other examples of teaching with historical perspectives. We believe that there is room for expanding THP beyond economics and are working towards a framework that could work across the disciplines.

NOTE

1.   This is the case, for example, of the debt deflation theory (Fisher, 1933) and of the new development economics, just to name a couple.

REFERENCES

Fisher, I. (1933), 'The debt-deflation theory of great depressions', *Econometrica*, **1**(4), 337–57, published in *Revue de l'Institut International de Statistique*, 1934, **1**(4), 48–65.

Freeman, A. (2007), 'Catechism versus pluralism: The heterodox response to the national undergraduate curriculum proposed by the UK Quality Assurance Authority', *Munich Personal RePEc Archive*, accessed 27 July 2017 at https://mpra.ub.uni-muenchen.de/6832/.

Garnett, R.F., Jr. (2009), 'Rethinking the pluralist agenda in economics education', *International Review of Economics Education*, **8**(2), 58–71, accessed 13 December 2017 at https://www.economicsnetwork.ac.uk/iree/v8n2/garnett.pdf.

Groenewegen, J. (2007), *Teaching Pluralism in Economics*, Cheltenham, UK and Northampton, MA, USA: Edward Elgar Publishing.

Sraffa, P. (1960), *The Production of Commodities by Means of Commodities*, Cambridge, UK: Cambridge University Press.

2. Integrating history of economic thought into introductory economics

Constantinos Repapis

1 INTRODUCTION

> A study in the history of opinion is a necessary preliminary to the emancipation of the mind. (Lord Keynes, 1926, *The End of Laissez-Faire*, I)

Since the crisis of 2007 there has been renewed interest in making the economics curriculum relevant to the events that are taking place on a global scale. This has provoked a variety of approaches, from student movements to institutional responses.[1] The plurality of approaches and responses has, in itself, been a substantial change to the prior situation when those responsible for undergraduate economic curricula, at least in the UK, have strived to increase uniformity not only in the approach to teaching economics, but also in the textbooks used. Therefore, some key textbooks, for example Mankiw's *Macroeconomics* (2015), or Varian's *Intermediate Microeconomics* (2014), had/have become the standard approach of these subjects in introductory and second-year courses, imposing a uniformity between universities that reaches even the recesses of specific examples and other incidental detail.

In this chapter I will not try to review, or assess, these broader issues concerning the systematic curriculum changes attempted in some institutions, but will focus on broadening the debate by adding another possible way forward. This is an attempt to see the history of economic thought (HET) as another way to renew and refresh the economics curriculum, and bring it in closer contact with the social and economic reality we live in. The previous sentence may appear to be founded on a contradiction. How could a field of study that appears both esoteric to the discipline and arcane, be a vehicle for making modern economics teaching rekindle its relation with the real world? The answer to this question can be summarized in the following way: by introducing context into the way we present both economic theory and the challenges of the modern economy.

The contextualization of economic ideas is the foundational principle of the history of economic thought. In fact, the very existence of this field of study arises from exactly an understanding of how economic ideas came about and what were the social/economic/political conditions that made these ideas both possible and popular. History of economic thought therefore includes as one of its central questions the relation of ideas to the times and conditions that gave rise to them. This is one way to reintroduce the link between economic reality and theory that emanates from the very centre of the economic tradition and has remained dormant in recent years. This could supplement other efforts to reinvigorate this link; efforts that focus on interdisciplinarity, or the introduction of new methods of analysis like case studies. These other ways to introduce context are not in competition with the introduction of a history of economic thought element into the curriculum, but would add strength and power to such an approach. It is my contention that the perspective of HET can act as an organizing centre for these other approaches to introducing realism to the economic curriculum, and in this short chapter I will explain how this can be done if we include topics from the history of ideas in a first-year undergraduate module on introductory economics.

The chapter is structured as follows. Section 2 discusses the issues that arise with introductory economics in current curricula, and makes a general argument on the use of the history of economic thought in a first-year introductory economics module. Section 3 reviews three past introductory economics 'anti-systemic' textbooks that had introduced HET in a substantial way. Section 4 presents an alternative suggestion for a first-year introductory economics module that uses the HET as its organizing centre. Section 5 concludes.

2 INTRODUCTORY ECONOMICS – THE FOUNDATIONS

Undergraduate university curricula usually have an introductory economics module that spans the first year of study. In some universities, there is a distinction between single honours and joint honours degrees, where single honours degrees have modules in introductory microeconomics and introductory macroeconomics, with joint honours putting the two together in one course of introductory economics. It is interesting to note that these differences usually serve purely administrative considerations – some universities prefer modules with a half-credit running for one semester; others prefer full-credit modules that run for a whole year. In single honours degrees there is also another augmentation: introductory micro/macro modules run for two semesters for full credit.

It is interesting to observe that this process, done rather routinely, immediately introduces the student to a division of the subject that is anything but straightforward. There is usually very little discussion or explanation of why this separation is natural or useful from the perspective of understanding the economy, or even the discipline of economics. It hides the fact that the division is itself a point of controversy, and different economists would take alternative positions on what types of questions these two domains of knowledge should encompass. Finally, there is very little explanation of why all foundational knowledge in economics must fall under either heading – micro or macro. What happens with topics that cannot fall easily under those headings, like economic methodology, economic history or the history of economic thought? These are not parvenu fields that cannot fit into an established rubric, but are fields that predate the rubric and can be seen as more foundational than the micro/macro divide itself. Any debate on the relation between microeconomic analysis and macroeconomic theory usually steps into a historical analysis of the evolution of the subject. An understanding of the evolution of microeconomics and macroeconomics, and the definitional or content controversies they are party to, is part of recreating the link between economic reality and the undergraduate rubric.

It is therefore important to start any reorientation of introductory economics by establishing the context of economic ideas, as a prequel to economic analysis rather than as an afterthought. Seen from this perspective, the first few lectures should be focusing on presenting the intellectual and historical context of our social reality, and the economic and the social questions that are important. This allows us to contextualize the most important questions of economics, which are: What is economics? What is its domain of analysis?

Most introductory economics textbooks start from a definition of economics that is very close to Lionel Robbins's original formulation as expressed in his 1935 book. A standard quote for Robbins's book would be: 'the science which studies human behaviour as a relationship between ends and scarce means which have alternative uses' (Robbins, 1935, p. 16). Occasionally the focus is not even so much on the problem of *choice*, but rather on the problem of *scarcity* itself, and choice is almost presented as a naturally occurring phenomenon whenever there is scarcity. Thus, Krugman and Wells note the following: 'A resource is scarce when there isn't enough of the resource available to satisfy all the ways a society wants to use it' (Krugman and Wells, 2013, p. 6). This confusion over the fundamentals of what is the foundational question of economics is both puzzling and revealing. It is puzzling because one would have thought that since there is so much broad agreement in introductory textbooks on what economics is, there would be a precise and well-expressed description of that definition, and an explanation of why this is the appropriate definition, possibly by investigating alternatives and showing their error. If we admit there is no precise definition that is beyond dispute, one would have expected introductory economics textbooks to have in their opening pages a discussion of what different economists make of their discipline and its content. The fact that introductory economics textbooks do not follow either procedure is revealing of a broader educational principle that is more controversial. This is that students should not be presented with different viewpoints other than alternatives in various stylized debates on specific issues. These alternatives are presented as contrasts that share the same basic understanding of the underlying real-world problem, and their differences are only positional, and not fundamental or to do with the perception of economic reality as such. Thus, for example, students will be presented with the problem of inflation versus unemployment in the macroeconomics parts of their textbook, and will learn that some people are more worried about unemployment than inflation, whereas others hold the opposite view. Viewpoints that do not fall on this axis are not presented. For example there are economists who question the use of unemployment as an aggregate index in itself, and others who do not find this tension exists, and even others who see no real analysis behind this construct but instead a game of rhetoric that allows the persistence of higher unemployment for entirely different reasons from those offered in the debate.

Therefore, this way of introducing debate does not introduce students to the problem of incommensurability of different viewpoints. They are not presented with the problem of economists disagreeing with what the key issues are, and the inherent complexity of reality that does not have an easy relation to the symbolic models and assumptions of introductory textbooks. Furthermore, it offers students a disservice, as it leads them to complete introductory economics modules with the implicit belief that all disputes in economics can be resolved by application to the same set of principles and methods, irrespective of the situation that they would have to deal with.

An appeal to the history of the subject could be a way to solve these issues without descending into incomprehension or a postmodernist view of the subject and its content. In fact, this would not be an introduction of new and untested principles, but instead an appeal to older ones that got lost in the process of change and standardization over the last 40 years. It is interesting to observe that a number of alternative introductory textbooks have made similar suggestions and have organized their material in this way in the past. In the next section I will concentrate on three examples that offer different ways of how such a reintegration can take place.

3   ALTERNATIVE INTRODUCTORY ECONOMICS TEXTBOOKS – A SELECTIVE HISTORY

There have been a substantial number of anti-systemic textbooks from the end of World War II until today. This literature is too large to review here; instead, my focus is the subset that reintroduced history of economic thought in a substantial way in their content. More specifically, I will focus on the following three introductory economics textbooks (in alphabetical order):[2]

- Cole, Cameron and Edwards ([1983] 1991), *Why Economists Disagree: The Political Economy of Economics*, second revised edition, London: Longman.
- Heilbroner and Thurow ([1968] 1981), *The Economic Problem*, sixth edition, Englewood Cliffs, NJ: Prentice Hall.
- Robinson and Eatwell ([1973] 1974), *An Introduction to Modern Economics*, revised edition, New York: McGraw-Hill.

Heilbroner's textbook is the earliest of the three, as it was single-authored in 1968, and later with Lester Thurow in 1975 for the fourth edition of the textbook. It was also commercially the most successful of the three, as it ran into seven editions, with the last one in 1984. By comparison, Robinson and Eatwell's textbook runs for only two editions (the first one in 1973 and a revised edition in 1974). Also, Cole, Cameron and Edwards's textbook was published twice, first in 1983 and second in 1991. These three textbooks, seen together, provided alternatives that included more substantial material from the history of economic thought for about a quarter of a century. Their structure and presentation of the topics is not only interesting as an exploration of this period's introductory economic textbooks, but can also guide us for the future integration of HET material in first-year curricula as well.

That Heilbroner's book was something different from the introductory textbooks that were available at the time can be attested to by contemporary book reviews. Groenewegen reviewed the book in *The Economic Record* and noted the following:

> This is a newcomer to the already overcrowded field of introductory economics texts for the use of schools and first-year university courses, and since its competitors include such established texts as Samuelson, Reynolds, Bach, Lipsey, etc., the reviewer is faced with the task of seeing whether this new entrant has something original to contribute which distinguishes it from the all-too-familiar pattern of basic micro and macro economics, preceded by a brief introduction on scope and method and followed by international economics and current problems. As is expected by a writer like Heilbronner [sic], this path is not followed, and although basic micro and macro, are, of course, included, together with international and current problems, the introduction is highly original. (Groenewegen, 1969, p. 138)

Groenewegen goes on to explain that 'Seven of the first eight chapters of the book (more than a quarter of the total volume) are devoted to economic history and the evolution of modern economic society' (ibid.). For Groenewegen, this was not only a break with current practices in the textbooks available circa 1968, but has been missing since the fifth edition of Marshall's *Principles* – the edition of Marshall's textbook that had economic history and history of economic thought in the beginning of the book rather than the appendixes that they occupied at the eighth edition. He continues, 'After Marshall, in any case, I know of no generally accepted textbook which has placed history in the foreground, until Heilbronner's [sic] book reached me' (Groenewegen, 1969, p. 139).

Although I will not trace the evolution of the book and its content from its first edition to the last, the following should be noted – by the sixth edition (1981) the introduction not only focused on economic history, but also key thinkers of this period. Thus, Chapter 2 was titled 'The Evolution of the Market System', and Chapter 3 was titled 'The Great Economists'. These two chapters work together, providing the strong historical framing effect that Groenewegen noted in his review. Thus, in Chapter 2 the following lines introduce the chapter: 'There is one central idea that this chapter will present – a very simple but exceedingly important idea. It is that capitalism – our Western economic society – represents a dramatic change in the way that mankind has grappled with its economic problems' (Heilbroner and Thurow [1968] 1981, p. 9). In Chapter 3 the introduction reads: 'The rise of one market system brought with it a great puzzle: to explain how such a system "worked" – what kept it together and in what direction it was headed. The name of this puzzle is economics' (Heilbroner and Thurow [1968] 1981, p. 27). Therefore, economics is introduced in its proper historical place and in an engaging fashion – as the discipline that developed to explain the dramatic changes that took place from the Industrial Revolution until today. This creates a link between reality and abstract theory that to some degree frames the remainder of the book. By introducing in Chapter 3 three key thinkers, Adam Smith, Karl Marx and John Maynard Keynes, the book by necessity introduces alternative world views of the economy, and this opens up spaces of competing interpretations of the social reality that would be missing from a more conventional text. This is even more forcefully pursued in the appendix to that chapter, which explores alternative paradigms in economics, and uses Thomas Kuhn's analysis to discuss historical changes from preclassical and classical economics to the marginalist and Keynesian revolutions. Nevertheless, by the sixth edition of Heilbroner and Thurow's book this framing exercise is not utilized extensively in the more standard part of the textbook, and in some ways the innovative element of the first few chapters appears to be soon forgotten. Thus, while Karl Marx and Adam Smith are introduced in Chapter 3, Marx is mentioned only twice and Smith only in a footnote reference in the next 600 pages.

Another example, and a – famously – more radical assault to the standard textbook, was the joint venture between Joan Robinson and

John Eatwell in the early 1970s. From the three textbooks discussed in this section this is the one that is more well known today among historians of the discipline. King and Millmow write the history of this textbook's publication and note in their introduction:

> This textbook was designed to revolutionize the teaching of elementary economics and to displace the influence of mainstream texts like those of Paul Samuelson and Richard Lipsey. Its lack of success marked something of a turning point in the history of economics, since it symbolized the collapse of the radical attempt to challenge orthodox theory at the pedagogical level. (King and Millmow, 2003, p. 105)

Furthermore, they note that 'The history of economic thought occupies 16.4 percent of Robinson and Eatwell but only 3.2 percent of Samuelson' (King and Millmow, 2003, p. 116). But this in itself is not the main difference between this book and Samuelson's, or other standard contemporary textbooks. The presentation and the arrangement of the material is substantially different, and this gave it the more radical thrust. King and Millmow undertake a content analysis between this textbook and the ninth edition of Samuelson's *Economics* ([1948] 1973) and find the following:

> He [Samuelson] begins with ten chapters of elementary theory, descriptive material, and institutional detail, and proceeds via the conventional macro and micro sections to distribution, the international economy, and a concluding section on 'current economic problems.' [Robinson and Eatwell's] *Introduction to Modern Economics* starts with three chapters on the history of economic thought, followed immediately by the analytical core of the text, the eleven theoretical chapters of part 2. Here, as befits a product of the Cambridge school, the micro and macro are thoroughly integrated… Thus the first two, apparently micro, chapters, titled 'Land and Labour' and 'Men and Machines,' already contain material on growth, income distribution, and money. They are followed by two essentially macro chapters on effective demand and technical change; an (almost) pure micro chapter on 'commodities and prices'; two mixed chapters on 'rates of profits' and 'incomes and demand'; a macro discussion of money and finance; chapter 9 on growth, which begins with the firm and moves first to the industry and then to the entire economy; a macro chapter on international issues; and a concluding chapter on socialist planning that again combines micro and macro problems. The only structural similarity with Samuelson comes in the third and final part of the book, which deals with the 'modern economic problems' of capitalism, socialism, and the Third World. (King and Millmow, 2003, p. 116)

What this extensive quote shows is that the Robinson and Eatwell book (for all its shortcomings, and King and Millmow review these extensively), takes a bolder step in using the framing that history of economic thought provides in substantially reorganizing the first-year material on less established lines. Furthermore, the HET part is substantially more detailed than in the sixth edition of the Heilbroner and Thurow book. In Robinson and Eatwell's book, Chapter 1 is titled 'Before Adam Smith', Chapter 2 'Classical Political Economy', and Chapter 3 'The Neoclassical Era'. These chapters are to a very large degree purely concerned with the analytical elements of these schools – not so much with the historical conditions that gave rise to them, other than noting the epoch as an aside. This is in marked contrast to Heilbroner and Thurow, which devoted equal weight to both history of economic thought and to the conditions of society during (and before) the Industrial Revolution – in the form of descriptive economic history. In contradistinction, Robinson and Eatwell use the HET section more extensively in the rest of their introductory textbook, and this is not only obvious by doing simple index accounting – Marx is mentioned in six pages outside the HET section, and this in a shorter book than Heilbroner and Thurow's – but also by the tenor of their arguments, which at times, follow analytical arguments that emanate from classical or other schools of thought.[3]

This naturally leads us to the third book under discussion by Cole, Cameron and Edwards. This is by far the less well known of these three textbooks, and it is also the most recent. It is also, I believe, the most idiosyncratic of the three and one that takes a step in a slightly different direction of organizing the first-year material on entirely new lines. Cole et al. start with the postulate that economics' basic purpose is to explain value. Then they use the history of economic thought as a device to build three competing systems of theoretical analysis. They call the first 'the subjective theory of value', the second 'the cost of production theory of value' and the third 'the abstract labour theory of value'. They find then that these three schools differ markedly in a range of aspects, from methodological to policy questions. An example of this comparison can be seen in Figure 2.1 at the end of the chapter. What is stressed continuously and becomes abundantly clear to the reader is that these different schools of thought are incommensurable in how they analyse the economy. For example, the authors note in the criticism levelled against Marx that he has no theory of prices:

[I]t is true, as we have stressed, that the derivation of prices is not the prime aim of the abstract labour theory, the main objective being the analysis of the dynamic of capitalism and of price formation by viewing capitalism at two levels – at the level of appearances (prices) and at the level of social relations (values). (Cole et al., 1983, p. 228)

This arraignment places modern micro theory in the first part of the book, that dealing with subjective theory of value, and distributes what would be considered as macro across different sections. But the important bottom line is that the micro/macro divide is not used at all, and indeed, what the book makes clear is that you can learn quite a lot of economics without even thinking that this is a useful partition of the material. This is not to say that the authors do not take sides – or have favourites among these three systems. But, what leanings there are in favour of one over the others can always be set within this frame of mind: it is simply the preference of the authors, and the reader can make up his or her own mind. More importantly, they do not try to synthesize a common ground that cannot be found. This is a new experience for the reader, who learns that different theories in economics can illuminate different aspects of the economy, and these are derived from fundamentally different views of the social and economic reality.[4] Here the link between theory and reality is multilevel. As Duhs notes in his book review: 'what Cole, Cameron and Edwards do very well ... is present an engaging account of the emerging evolution of economic thought in the context of the broadly based understanding of the emerging social, political, and philosophical issues of the day' (Duhs, 1985, p. 253). But this is only one aspect of the relation between theory and reality. More substantially, by introducing alternative – incommensurable – viewpoints, the reader is naturally led to be reflective about his or her own use of the economic tools when confronting a real situation, and the deep political nature of economic questions. Whether this is a liberating or simply a confusing experience for the reader/ student, is a deep issue that has clear educational ramifications. And even if we agree that it is in principle a liberating experience and, a necessary one if we want to produce economists who are citizens in democratic societies and are aware of the bias of their arguments, it may well hold dangers, both in asking too much from the first-year undergraduate student, and in creating a narrative that comes close to post-modernism – that is, any viewpoint can be defended, and there are no wrong answers. This problem is one of the issues that a more pluralist approach always has to deal with, and in this case it is solved by using lineages from the history of the subject. An example of this method can be seen in Figure 2.2 at the end of the chapter (reproduced from Cole et al., 1983, p. 16).[5]

4   AN ALTERNATIVE SUGGESTION FOR TEACHING INTRODUCTORY ECONOMICS WITH HET

Goldsmiths, University of London, recently began a new under-graduate degree in Economics (BA), to supplement its current under-graduate offering in Philosophy, Politics and Economics (BA), and Economics, Politics and Public Policy (BA). Furthermore, its new BA Economics degree introduces students both to interdisciplinary perspectives and to alternative theoretical paradigms within econom-ics. These degrees necessitated a first-year introductory economics module that could cater for a very diverse audience in background and motivation. Thus, the sequence of lectures and topics developed in introductory economics intends to present students with both the broader political contours of economic analysis, and lay the analyti-cal foundations for those students that would continue with the more technical economics degree. Table 2.1 at the end of the chapter shows the topics that are covered in the 20 weekly two-hour lectures divided into the two terms.

What this sequence of lectures shows is that the year is broadly divided into three sections. After an introductory week, students have five weeks of economic history/history of economic thought before going into eight weeks of microeconomic theory, and finally six weeks of macroeconomics. The first five-week sequence begins with a lecture on the development of the modern economy, and intends to explain that many features of our social and economic reality are the outcome of the Industrial Revolution and the market economy that came onto the scene in the eighteenth century. This immediately provides historical context for the whole module, anchoring the ana-lytical developments of economics within a specific period of human history.

This counterpoint between developments in abstract theory and social/economic conditions is further strengthened in the next four weeks, where the following economists are discussed in sequence:

Adam Smith, David Ricardo, Karl Marx and Alfred Marshall. These four weeks present economics through its 'system builders' – theorists that strand the nineteenth and early twentieth centuries and develop their own broad and comprehensive picture of how the economy works. Each lecture starts by presenting the person's lifetime, his times, and the methodology by which he tries to understand the economic and social reality before discussing some analytical arguments that emanate from his work. This focus on individual economists may appear as too biographical, but it has certain useful features. First, it introduces students to how economists try to create abstract arguments from observing the world around them – and few economists had been more successful in creating and projecting their abstractions to the profession than the four economists noted above. Second, it introduces students to alternative methodologies and approaches of doing abstract analysis in economics. Third, it introduces students to alternative schools of economic thought through their founders. This solves a number of problems. It gives plurality some structure, as students understand that the key thinkers have developed a whole system of analysis, and this system is both complex and has defined limits on what it intends to – and can – explain. It also does not set a specific linear history of how these theorists relate to modern schools of thought, and the thinkers in the interim that ascribe to this or that school, as attempted in Cole et al.'s textbook.

This sequence of economists ends with Alfred Marshall, which acts as a bridge to modern microeconomic analysis. Then students have five weeks that covers standard microeconomic topics, like consumer theory (axioms of preference, utility curves, etc.) and the theory of the firm (cost curves, perfect competition, monopoly, monopolistic competition). But even within these standard weeks the historical framework can be utilized in a variety of ways to give context to standard analysis. For example, at the end of three weeks of neoclassical choice, students in other universities are sometimes presented with some criticisms of this theory, and this is also the case here. The criticism presented is by Thorstein Veblen and his *Theory of the Leisure Class* ([1899] 1957). This work is not only an alternative understanding of consumption behaviour based on a class analysis of society, but also Veblen, a contemporary of Marshall, is seen as someone who analysed society on very different lines to Marshall, and the contrast is pointed out. Veblen's work is presented not only as criticism of neoclassical, individualistic, rational choice theory, but as foundational to an alternative understanding of consumption behaviour, drawn on very different lines. This contrast is also utilized when presenting perfect competition – the student is introduced to Sraffa's (1926) critique before being introduced to monopoly and monopolistic competition.[6] The broader question here is whether market economies broadly tend towards competition or concentration – a question that links this technical discussion with the previous presentation of Marshall and Marx. Therefore, the point of these two contrasts is to discuss the overall utility of neoclassical theory in understanding social reality, and to briefly introduce alternative paradigms. Thus, students can ponder questions of the following kind: Is consumption primarily determined by rational individual behaviour or more of a social phenomenon? Is most production taking place in an environment of perfect competition or of other market structures?

These questions are given their final articulation in the last three weeks of microeconomic analysis, which is on partial and general equilibrium. The last topics presented are the two welfare theorems, and this closes a conceptual journey that started with Adam Smith and the presentation of the invisible hand and the virtues of exchange more than ten weeks before. Thus, students can see how neoclassical economists have come to the final rigorous analytical articulation of the concept of the invisible hand and the assumptions that are needed to make it work. Microeconomics ends with some questions: What do the welfare theorems tell us? Are they descriptive of the economy, or prescriptive of what we should aspire the economy to achieve? Or do they tell us something else? These questions have no definite answer, and the students are asked to think for themselves on the broad relation between central findings in economic theory and the economic and social reality of today.

The final part of the module deals with macroeconomics. These final six weeks start with a discussion on the relation between microeconomics and macroeconomics, and the issues that arise from this. This sets the stage for the polyphony that usually takes place in macroeconomic discourse between different policy recommendations and the models that gave rise to them. In this module, in the first four weeks, students are presented with introductory remarks on the usual array of topics: aggregate indexes and national accounting, money and banking, growth and the real economy, aggregate demand/aggregate supply (AD/AS). The difference here is that in each week students are also presented with a school of thought that is mostly associated with that topic. Thus, the first week sees a brief presentation of J.M. Keynes and the post-Keynesian school, the second a presentation of monetarism and the Austrians, the third an introduction to real business cycle theory, and the fourth an introduction to new Keynesian microfoundations models.

After these four weeks where students are introduced both to the central topics of macroeconomics and the main features of some macroeconomic schools of thought, they can start using these tools in important debates, which occupy the final two weeks of the introductory economics module. The first of these weeks is on the relation between inflation and unemployment, and students are presented with the variety of viewpoints that these schools have on this topic. The focus here is not to synthesize a common ground but instead to show that these topics are viewed very differently by these competing schools of macroeconomic thought.

Finally, the last week is titled 'Business Cycles or Economic Crises?' and this completes the intellectual journey that started at the beginning of the module with the questions of what is this new type of society that has come into existence from the Industrial Revolution until today, how is it organized, and what are the issues of this new organization? One central question in all this is whether this new system of consumption, production and exchange is prone to crises or, more generally what are we to make of these crises or cycles that seem to be a recurrent phenomenon? Here we have a topic of discussion that extends beyond macroeconomics and reaches as far back as the classical economists. Students can use the different narratives that have been built since the beginning of the module to articulate an opinion and also see the range of opinion on this topic. It is in this last week that this whole alternative scheme comes to a conclusion that utilizes all the elements of the course, and sets old opinion on the same footing as contemporary ones and asks students to discuss and debate these viewpoints. This shows that a history of economic thought section not only adds historical colour to an introductory economics module, but also opens up the range of opinion that the student gets exposed to, introducing an element of pluralism that emanates from the very core of the discipline.

5   CONCLUSION

The central questions that this chapter tried to answer are: Why use topics from the history of economic thought in introductory economic modules? And how can this be done? The answers to these questions are not easy and depend on the motivation behind introducing topics from the history of the subject into the curriculum. A central question is whether one believes in a Whig history of economics, in which topics from the history of the subject are simply 'crowding out' material from the forefront of the discipline without adding anything. The other view is that the history of the subject can be used as a vehicle to introduce alternative viewpoints. Boulding, in his classic paper 'After Samuelson, Who Needs Adam Smith?' (1971) makes the argument in favour of the second option by utilizing the principle of the extended present. This principle argues that there is a period of time in which core understandings of a discipline are still evolving, and from which alternative viewpoints can be drawn. Boulding argues that books like Smith's (1776) *The Wealth of Nations* are part of the extended present, as they provide economists with new avenues of thought and research, which cannot be arrived at from contemporary models. This achieves a plurality of viewpoints that is unavailable to someone only studying the latest models. Thus, Boulding argues: 'the Principle seems to me pretty clear that as long as intellectual evolutionary potential remains yet undeveloped in the early writers, the modern writers are a complement rather than a substitute' (Boulding, 1971, p. 231). This quote answers both the why and how this can be done. The application of this principle was the main argument of the third section, where three introductory textbooks that implicitly utilized this principle were discussed, and the fourth section where an alternative introductory economics module was mapped out. These four viewpoints show that there can be many markedly different ways of introducing HET into the curriculum, and it would go against the very nature of the argument here if it were proposed that the current monophony of introductory economics should be replaced by a new one that inserts HET in one specific way into introductory modules. If pluralism is a guiding principle, then it means not only the presentation of alternatives within a programme of studies or a module, but also alternatives between universities and in this case introductory economics courses. This could better utilize the different capacities and knowledge lecturers have, and provide prospective undergraduate students with a menu of options to choose from instead of one standardized product. That the creation of choice is welfare improving is a central result of neoclassical consumer theory for all products, and maybe it is time that the argument should be extended to the economics curriculum as well.

NOTES

1. There is an expanding literature on this topic, which cannot be surveyed here. A start may be Sheehan, Embery and Morgan (2015), Morgan (2015) or Reardon and Madi (2014), which review current mainstream institutional changes from a critical perspective. Also, this chapter does not review the CORE textbook advanced by a number of mainstream economists as an alternative textbook to existing introductory textbooks. It has been noted before (discussion in the plenary session of the European Society in the History of Economic Thought, XIX Annual Conference, Roma-Tre University, May 2015, and in Morgan, 2015, pp. 19–22) that this textbook introduces history of economic thought in a limited way, as key economists, like David Ricardo or Karl Marx, are given a very brief introduction in a textbox, and they are – at best – referred to briefly in other sections. It does not have a whole section on the history of economic thought, as such, nor does it present alternative economists as developing different systems of thought. Furthermore, it has been discussed extensively in the critical literature noted above. For these reasons, I do not review this textbook here, but the reader can find further information and the textbook at http://www.core-econ.org/.
2. This is not a complete list of all introductory textbooks that have a strong historical and HET element. For example, Sherman et al. ([2007] 2015), *Economics: An Introduction to Traditional and Progressive Views*, seventh edition, is not reviewed here. (Before that, two of the authors, Sherman and Hunt, wrote *Economics: An Introduction to Traditional and Radical Views*, first edition, 1972; sixth edition, 1990. The first edition is discussed in King and Millmow, 2003.) The 2015 edition starts with two sections on the 'Economics of History and History of Economics', before discussing macro- and microeconomics. This seventh edition and its earlier version has been more of a success than the three textbooks reviewed in this section. I do not focus on this textbook as it is still available for academics to use and set as a text for students taking introductory economics. Instead, I focus on three textbooks that are no longer in print but have some attractive characteristics from the perspective of this chapter's thesis.
3. On this, King and Millmow write 'They [Robinson and Eatwell] had also integrated theory and history, analysis and institutions, giving their text a strong "comparative systems" orientation' (King and Millmow, 2003, p. 127).
4. That this is a foundational aspect of this book can be seen not only from the title, but also from the following quote with which the book ends: 'Our aim in this book has not been to stifle or preclude such theoretical debates but to provide a framework in which all the vital discussions of today can be understood and that many more people can actively participate in them. A greater understanding of one's own implied basic principles and those of opponents is crucial to such participation' (Cole et al., 1983, p. 289).

Summary 1.3

Economics rises with the market against vested interests — 3 schools develop

	Determination of value	Political conflict	Political institutions	Theory of social change	Theory of science
Subjective preference theory of value	Individual utility: value determined in consumption	No conflict if free exchange	Representative state which assures free exchange	Development and acceptance of new ideas	Falsification (Popper): economics as a separate discipline
Cost-of production theory of value	Technology and distribution: value determined in production	Conflict over distribution	Pluralist state intervenes to harmonise competing interests	Evolutionary development of technology	Paradigms (Kuhn): multi-disciplinarity
Abstract labour theory of value	Social relations of production: theory historically specific	Conflict fundamental to society	State reflects and reinforces class power	Class conflict leads to revolutionary change	Political action: inter-disciplinarity

Source: Cole, Cameron and Edwards (1983), *Why Economists Disagree: The Political Economy of Economics*, London: Longman, p. 20.

Figure 2.1 Three theories of value and their differences in Cole, Cameron and Edwards (1983)

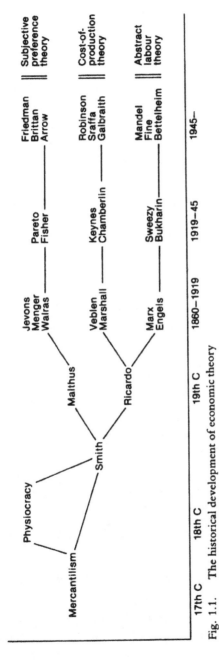

Fig. 1.1.   The historical development of economic theory

Source: Cole, Cameron and Edwards (1983), *Why Economists Disagree: The Political Economy of Economics*, London: Longman, p. 16.

Figure 2.2   The historical development of the three theories of value in Cole, Cameron and Edwards (1983)

Table 2.1 Introductory Economics (30 credits) at Goldsmiths, University of London

Term (Semester) 1	Term (Semester) 2
Week 1 – What is Economics? Students are introduced to alternative perspectives on what economics is from mainstream and heterodox texts *Week 2 – What is a Market Economy?* Students are presented with a brief economic history of Western Europe, and the importance of the Industrial Revolution. It is indicated that economics, as a discipline, developed to explain these unprecedented social and economic changes *Week 3 – Adam Smith* Introduction to key aspects of the *Wealth of Nations*, especially the division of labour, the extent of the market and the human inclination to exchange *Week 4 – David Ricardo* Introduction to the corn model and the theory of comparative advantage. Students learn about the three classes in Ricardo – landowners, workers and capitalists *Week 5– Karl Marx* Introduction to key aspects of Marx's thought, including his theory of value, stages of socioeconomic development, and the contradictions of capitalism	*Week 1 – Producer's Problem – Competitive Firms* Sraffa's 1926 article and departures from perfect competition that do not involve strategic interaction: monopoly, monopolistic competition *Week 2 – Supply/Demand and Partial Equilibrium Welfare Analysis* Students are introduced to the following: consumer and producer surplus, government intervention and welfare analysis: taxation, quantity restrictions, price floor/ceiling Definition of an ideal market *Week 3 – General Equilibrium I* Introduction to pure exchange between two individuals (Edgeworth box) Difference between partial/general equilibrium First welfare theorem *Week 4 – General Equilibrium II* First hour: second welfare theorem. What is the meaning of the welfare theorems? Descriptive, prescriptive or something else? Second hour: the relation between micro and macro *Week 5 – The Modern Macroeconomy* Topics covered: introduction, national accounting, macroeconomic aggregates Presentation of school of thought: J.M. Keynes and post-Keynesian theory

Term (Semester) 1	Term (Semester) 2
Week 6 – Alfred Marshall *Principles of Economics*, the small-scale producer responding to market changes Introduction to the following concepts: normative/positive, opportunity cost, Pareto principle, supply/demand *Week 7 – Consumer Theory I* Marshall was the link with modern microanalysis, and this week preference theory, budget constraints, and graphical construction of utility curves are covered *Week 8 – Consumer Theory II* Students are introduced to income and substitution effects, and then to neoclassical theory (labour–leisure decision) of providing labour to the competitive market *Week 9 – Consumer Theory III* First hour: students are introduced to intertemporal neoclassical consumer choice Second hour: criticism of neoclassical consumer choice through the work of Thorstein Veblen (esp. *The Theory of the Leisure Class*) *Week 10 – Producer's Problem– Costs of Firms* Introduction to cost curves, and the maximization problem of a small competitive firm. The concepts of returns to scale and minimum efficient scale are presented and critically discussed	*Week 6 – Money and Banking* Topics: what is money, quantity theory of money, demand for money Presentation of two schools of thought: (1) monetarism; (2) Austrians *Week 7 – Growth and the Real Economy* Topics: Solow growth model, rational expectations Presentation of school of thought: real business cycles *Week 8 – Aggregate Fluctuations – AS/AD* Topic: short-run vs long-run AS/AD Presentation of school of thought: new Keynesian microfoundation models *Week 9 – Macroeconomic Debate I: Inflation/Unemployment* Topics: inflation or unemployment? A trade-off? Views from the various schools of thought: different framing of the problem depending on the school of macroeconomic thought *Week 10 – Macroeconomic Debate II: Business Cycles/Economic Crises* Topics: business cycles or economic crises? Are they the same thing? An exploration of the problem of crises from Ricardo and Marx to real business cycles

1Teaching the history of economic thought

5. The problem of post-modernism is dealt successfully in Cole et al.'s book, by stressing that there are only three theories of value and describing these three in analytical detail. By creating complete systems, with exact historical lineages, the reader is aware of pluralism without going into an 'anything goes' narrative. But, this approach has weaknesses. That the construction of these histories leads to an occasionally controversial placement of theorists to fit the broader rubric is an aspect that can make some historians of economic thought (including me) uneasy. What I mean by this can be seen in Figure 2.2 and the groupings of prominent economists there.
6. This has been suggested by Avi Cohen. See Cohen (1996).

REFERENCES

Boulding, K.E. (1971), 'After Samuelson, who needs Adam Smith?', *History of Political Economy*, **3**(2), 225–37.

Cohen, A.J. (1996), 'Why haven't textbooks resolved Sraffa's 1926 complaints?', in *Rethinking Economic Principles*, Chicago, IL: Irwin, pp. 81–91.

Cole, K., J. Cameron and C. Edwards (1983), *Why Economists Disagree: The Political Economy of Economics*, London: Longman.

Cole, K., J. Cameron and C. Edwards ([1983] 1991), *Why Economists Disagree: The Political Economy of Economics*, second revised edition, London: Longman.

CORE (2017), *The Economy: Economics for a Changing World*, first edition. Oxford: Oxford University Press. Also available as an e-book at http://www.core-econ.org/the-economy/, last accessed 21 December 2017.

Duhs, L.A. (1985), 'Book review of "Why Economists Disagree: The Political Economy of Economics"', *Journal of Economic Issues*, **19**(1), 252–55.

Groenewegen, P.D. (1969), 'Book review of "The Economic Problem" by R.L. Heilbronner [sic]', *The Economic Record*, 138–9.

Heilbroner, R.L. and L.C. Thurow ([1968] 1981), *The Economic Problem*, sixth edition, Englewood Cliffs, NJ: Prentice Hall.

Keynes, J.M. (1926), *The End of Laissez-Faire*, London: Hogarth Press.

King, J.E. and A. Millmow (2003), 'Death of a revolutionary textbook', *History of Political Economy*, **35**(1), 105–34.

Krugman, P. and R. Wells (2013), *Economics*, third edition, New York: Worth.

Mankiw, G. (2015), *Macroeconomics*, ninth revised edition, London: Palgrave Macmillan.

Marshall, A. (1961), *Principles of Economics*, 2 volumes, ninth variorum edition, London: Macmillan.

Morgan, J. (2015), 'Pluralism, heterodoxy, and the prospects for a new economics curriculum: Assessing the potential of INET, *What's the Use of Economics*, and the CORE project', Association for Heterodox Economics, accessed 13 December 2017 at https://www.researchgate.net/profile/

Jamie_Morgan3/publication/275516890_Pluralism_Heterodoxy_and_the_prospects_for_a_new_economics_curriculum_Assessing_the_potential_of_INET_What's_the_Use_of_Economics_and_the_CORE_project/links/55 3de81e0cf2c415bb0f80aa.pdf.

Reardon, J. and M.A. Madi (eds) (2014), 'Introduction', in *The Economics Curriculum: Towards a Radical Reformulation*, Milton Keynes: World Economics Association, pp. 3–12.

Robbins, L. (1935), *An Essay on the Nature and Significance of Economic Science*, second edition, London: Macmillan.

Robinson, J. and J. Eatwell ([1973] 1974), *An Introduction to Modern Economics*, second revised edition, New York: McGraw-Hill.

Samuelson, P.A. ([1948] 1973), *Economics*, ninth edition, New York: McGraw-Hill.

Sheehan, B., J. Embery and J. Morgan (2015), 'Give them something to think about, don't tell them what to think: A constructive heterodox alternative to the CORE project', *The Journal of Australian Political Economy*, **75**, 211–32.

Sherman, H.J., E.K. Hunt, R.E. Nesiba, P. O'Hara and B. Wiens-Tuers ([2007] 2015), *Economics: An Introduction to Traditional and Progressive Views*, seventh edition, London: Routledge.

Smith, A. (1776), *An Inquiry into the Nature and Causes of the Wealth of Nations*, London: W. Strahan and T. Cadell.

Sraffa, P. (1926), 'The laws of returns under competitive conditions', *Economic Journal*, **36**(4), 535–50.

Varian, H. (2014), *Intermediate Microeconomics: A Modern Approach*, ninth international student edition, New York: W.W. Norton & Company.

Veblen, T.B. ([1899] 1957), *The Theory of the Leisure Class*, London: Allen and Unwin.

3. Teaching economic theory based on the history of economic thought

Joseph Halevi

1 INTRODUCTION

When in June 2016 Dr Daniela Tavasci approached me to ask whether I would be interested in writing a chapter on the volume's theme, I was, having just retired, coming out of one of the most significant pedagogical experiences in my 40 years of teaching, spread over several institutions. In 2004, I founded, and taught till retirement, the main second-year economic theory course at the newly established Department of Political Economy at the University of Sydney: Economic Theories of Modern Capitalism, code ECOP2011. The Department, which was formed in 2000, originated from a split within the traditional Economics Department in the 1970s. Although its main focus is on issues and not on analytical approaches to economics, its creation provided the opportunity for establishing a mainstay course based on a comprehensive historical and analytical view of economics from its modern inception. ECOP2011 could not have been developed inside any standard department regardless of the serious limitations of Sydney's then Department of Political Economy. At best, it would have been relegated to the status of an elective unit.

2 SOME PRELIMINARY ARGUMENTS IN FAVOUR OF THE INTEGRATION OF HISTORY OF ECONOMIC THOUGHT WITH ECONOMIC THEORY AND VICE VERSA

Mainstream core courses are organized around first-year Introductory micro- and macroeconomics and a second year of exactly the same thing, only with more graphs and with the added label 'Intermediate'. The relevant textbooks embody the restrictive pedagogical assumption that there is nothing to learn from past theories except for those pieces acting as foundational elements of the current doctrine, such as preference sets, the upward- and downward-sloping supply and demand curves, Edgeworth box, and so on. Superficially, the texts appear to follow the scientific criterion of incorporating from the past what is still objectively relevant to the discipline. However, such an approach to economics is definitely harmful, while it is not advisable even in relation to the real sciences.[1]

Let us take the Keynesian revolution as an example. Keynes's contribution can be seen as a conscious, albeit imperfect, break from the microeconomic foundations of the pre-existing neoclassical theory. The *General Theory of Employment, Interest and Money* (1936) constituted a paradigm change relative to the dominant doctrines; it was not just the expression of the emergence of a new field of study called macroeconomics. The essence of that theoretical shift lies in that price and wage flexibilities do not determine the attainment of the full employment level of output, nor does saving combine with investment via the adjustment of the interest rate treated as a real price. This type of perspective never arises in traditional texts, although it has been the basis of the whole Keynes-Robinson-Pasinetti-Harcourt Cantabrian-Italian school (Harcourt, 2006; Pasinetti, 2007). The maturity of a discipline is validated when its internal debates and practices enable researchers to become aware of the need for a paradigm change should the received doctrines end, as often happens, in a blind alley. In this respect, mainstream economics does not pass the test.

Past ideas that appear to have been discarded may still have validity depending upon historical circumstances. Economics, as Gunnar Myrdal (1953) taught us long ago, always contains a political element. Hence, theories might have been jettisoned not because they were being superseded by better ones, but rather for ideological reasons. Placing economic theory within the framework of history of economic thought as well as treating the latter in a theoretical-oriented dimension, therefore becomes a necessary condition for empowering students to evaluate, filter and sift through their subject matter.

A typical mainstream anti-intellectual pedagogic attitude emanates from Olivier Blanchard's intervention in the heated debate that from 2000 to 2002 accompanied the Parisian students' struggle for a change in the teaching curricula in favour, *inter alia*, of greater emphasis on the history of economics. The already world-famous Franco-MIT economist waded into the discussion in defence of the traditional programme with an article in the daily newspaper *Libération*:

> A bit of history of economic thought may be useful here. More than two hundred years ago Adam Smith explained that, in a market economy, individualistic egoisms combined in such a way as to bring about the best possible collective outcome. The proposition was so striking and so heavily loaded with consequences, that understanding its nature and its limits became paramount. Thanks to Walras, at the beginning of the twentieth century and, 50 years later, thanks to economists like Arrow or Debreu, and above all thanks to an enormous effort of abstraction and to the utilization of powerful mathematical tools, the conditions underlying Adam Smith's theorem have been clarified. (Blanchard, 2000; my translation from French)

The above passage captures perfectly what is wrong with contemporary economic teaching based on the marginalization and, increasingly, on the elimination of the history of economic thought from the curriculum. By presenting himself as someone knowledgeable in the history of ideas, Blanchard leads the reader to believe that there is a conceptual continuity between Adam Smith and contemporary general equilibrium theory. The sleight of hand consists in that the MIT academic chose to ignore the fact – well established by the historians of the discipline – that there is hardly any connection between Adam Smith's reference to an invisible hand and the multimarket intertemporal equilibrium framework of Arrow and Debreu. At the epistemological level, an indirect – that is, not specifically related to Blanchard's article – yet accurate rebuttal came from Alessandro Roncaglia:

> Among contemporary economists the idea is widespread that general economic equilibrium theory is to be identified with theory *tout court*, and is to be taken as a yardstick by which any other theory can be considered as a particular case. To anyone sharing this viewpoint, the history of economic thought appears as the path of progressive development and consolidation of this theory. Along this route, in interpreting classical economists, the economic issue they dealt with is identified in the functioning of the 'invisible hand of the market'. The latter would ensure not simply a sufficiently regular working of the economy but

also, more than this, a systematic tendency towards an equilibrium with perfect equality between supply and demand for each commodity (market clearing), even in the presence of many commodities and many economic agents. As a matter of fact, such an extreme idea cannot be attributed to the economists of the classical period; it was originally developed by only one of the 'schools' that concurred in the so-called marginalist revolution, the 'Lausanne school', founded by Léon Walras. (Roncaglia, 2005, p. 322)

At times of political and cultural confrontation, as was the case in France 17 years ago, references to the history of economic ideas will always surface, since the economic foundations of a society are among the first elements to come under criticism. Making the study and the knowledge of the history of ideas available to the entire body of students therefore becomes an essential democratic requirement for also empowering the public at large.

2.1   The French Origins of ECOP2011: The Experiment with *Modélisation*

I designed the Sydney course in 2003 when I was at the University of Grenoble in France. There, for many years, I taught a third-year course called *Modélisation* – that is, modelling – which I transformed into a course on growth theories. I followed advice given to me by my close friend and colleague Redouane Taouil, who is a very fine theorist and epistemologist. Taouil observed that through growth theory one can identify the essence as well as the main problems of economic doctrines and of their evolution through time. The implementation of *Modélisation* was made possible by the fact that the Grenoble department was heterodox in its academic orientation, with, however, a high degree of theoretical emphasis, and with an interest in the economic history of production cycles, in statistics as well as in international monetary economics and, last but not least, in the history of economic thought. The curriculum included mathematical economics and econometrics, which made the teaching of growth models easier.

The Grenoble experience taught me that it is quite possible to combine the history of economics with systematic theoretical modelling. I benefited from the methodology developed by Vivian Walsh and Harvey Gram in their exquisitely elegant book *Classical and Neoclassical Theories of General Equilibrium: Historical Origins and Mathematical Structure* (1980). The authors build two different linear models based on two commodities. One operates in a classical manner, while the second is a land-and-labour, wheat-and-rice neoclassical model of general equilibrium where, therefore, endowments are given. They widen the theoretical structure by introducing into the classical model neoclassical demand conditions and then show that these do not alter the cost of production foundations of classical price theory. Furthermore, when the above theoretical exercise is viewed in conjunction with the authors' historical analysis regarding the formation of both strands, it becomes possible to see that the newer strand is not a further advance on the older one. Instead, it expresses an altogether different conception of economic activity. For the classics, the economic process is a circular one with a correspondence between income categories, social classes and the structure of production. This circular process 'stands in striking contrast to the view presented by modern theory of a one-way avenue that leads from "Factors of production" to "Consumption goods"' (Sraffa, 1960, p. 93).

3   TEACHING 'ECONOMIC THEORIES OF MODERN CAPITALISM' AT THE UNIVERSITY OF SYDNEY: FIRST HALF – FROM THE PHYSIOCRATS TO KEYNES AND KALECKI

While planning for ECOP2011, I established the following objectives. First, students are to become knowledgeable of the fact that there are several fully mature economic theories. These, however, are not freely competing paradigms but often stand as adversaries in relation to each other, where the dominance of one is frequently determined by a process involving ideology and the intervention of institutions. A clear example is the way in which the textbook written after World War II by Lorie Tarshis and Stephenson Furniss (1947) was banned in favour of Samuelson's first edition of *Economics* (1948). Second, students should be aware both of the context in which the theoretical approaches had been developed and the crucial flaws contained in each.

I dealt with the subjects by trying to highlight the reasons for the fundamental failures in each group of theories; Keynes, however, was spared, since, as I told the class, his non-deterministic way of think-ing should be considered path-breaking. Relative to the Grenoble experience, the Sydney one had a major drawback in that only a small minority of students possessed an acceptable mathematical background. Yet, the lack of mathematics created a new challenge: the excellent head tutor Dr Roni Demirbag and I decided to find the most concise forms to express, when required, the analytical features of the theories discussed. This procedure helped us identify a common critical thread that would run throughout the course: namely, beyond the single-sector/single-agent/single-technique models, the theories concerned perform rather badly. Throughout the discipline's history – from Ricardo, to Marx, to Wicksell, to Samuelson, to Lucas – attempts to generalize from the single case to a multiplicity of instances have, more often than not, encountered unsurmountable obstacles.

The course entailed a class of between 180 and 220 second-year students during the years in which it was compulsory. A large number of tutorial groups was required, each made up of 15–18 students taught by a team of up to three tutors. The course was divided into two equal halves. The first dealt with three groups of theories: classical economics, marginalist (neoclassical) economics, Keynesian and Kaleckian economics. The second half was based on two sections. The first focused on the post-1945 neoclassical repossession of Keynes through the Hicks–Modigliani IS–LM appa-ratus, as well as on Solow's growth model, both forming the core of the MIT ideology. The section ended by showing the collapse of the Keynesian–neoclassical synthesis by analytically using the Cambridge UK capital debate and Joan Robinson's (1972) argu-ments regarding the real reasons why a second crisis in economics set in by the end of the 1960s. The second section treated the rise and the theoretical decline of the theory of rational expectations. The course ended by looking at the efficient market hypothesis (EMH) and at the dynamic stochastic general equilibrium models (DSGE), thanks to the publication of John Quiggin's (2012) book, which was much appreciated by the students. No text was used, only chapters from different textbooks were assigned. Lecture notes were made electronically available for each of the 13 weeks. The reading material for both lectures and tutorials was updated yearly, put online and bound in a hard-copy reading kit of 550 pages.

3.1   How the Course Unfolded: Classical Economics

The classical part of the first half of the course started with Marx's characterization of the physiocrats as the thinkers who put political economy on a scientific footing. Economic relations are objective and, to paraphrase William Petty, independent of the opinions and appetites of particular 'men'. François Quesnay's *tableau économique* is presented to evince both the formation of the annual agricultural surplus and the input–output nature of the economy. Students are then transported into modern times since they are taught the genesis of the Leontief's system and its application in the UN World Tables. Marx's interpretation of the physiocrats' limits, resulting from their looking at capitalist production in a feudal setting, becomes the ramp from which to access the British classical economists, where surplus and accumulation appear more fully in their capitalistic light. The text guiding us from the physiocrats to Ricardo – but not to Smith – and to Marx's labour theory of value is the first chapter of Luigi Pasinetti's *Lectures* (1977), which contains an extremely accessible presentation of the *tableau économique*, of Pasinetti's own model of Ricardo's theory of distribution and accumulation, and a most didactically valuable introduction to Marx's production and value theory. There the links between Marx and the physiocrats and between Marx and Ricardo can easily be learned.

Adam Smith is introduced in a twofold manner. The Smithian notion of competition, based on free entry and exit in each industry, leading to a uniform rate of profits, is taught in order to highlight the difference between the classics and the neoclassics where, for the latter, perfect competition implies an infinitely large number of small firms operating at diminishing returns. A seminal paper by Paolo Sylos Labini (1984a) is used to underline the relevance of Adam Smith's dynamics as well as his choice of a labour-commanded measure of value that, in Sylos Labini's interpretation, makes the Scottish thinker relevant for the analysis of different social systems. The second aspect of Smith's treatment deals with the corn growth model. The goal is to signal the importance for classical theory of Smith's statement whereby 'every frugal man [is] a public benefactor'. In this single-product world, savings are unconsumed corn that must be invested as there is no reason for it to rot in barnyards. Students are asked to read an excellent chapter by John Hicks (1965, ch. 4) titled 'Primitive Growth Models: Smith and Ricardo'. Primitive because, paraphrasing Adam Smith, parsimony rather than industry is the immediate cause of the increase in capital. This leads to the establishment of a connection with Max Weber's view of capitalism propelled by thriftiness stemming from Protestant ethics. However, no sooner do we finish illustrating the Smith–Weber similarity, students' attention is directed toward the issue of effective demand. The latter arises straightforwardly as soon as investment goods are taken to be physically different from consumption goods, entailing the explicit introduction of money into the system.

Understanding the nature of the corn model allows for a smooth progression onto Ricardo and Marx. It is emphasized that in Ricardo the central issue is the theory of distribution in favour of profits against landowners. Via Pasinetti (1977, ch. 1) and Sraffa's introduction to Ricardo's *Essay on Profits* (1815) we point out that Ricardo's conclusions are impeccable. Trouble arises when more than one commodity is involved. Ricardo's solution was the adoption of the labour theory of value where long-period relative prices are equal to the amount of time bestowed on the production of each commodity. Students are at this point requested to fully incorporate into their learning that Ricardo's argument remains valid only if: (1) commodities are produced by labour alone, as already pointed out by Adam Smith who, therefore, opted for a labour-commanded theory of value; and (2) capital inputs are equiproportional.

We then address the way in which the issues reappear in Marx. Yet, the study of Marx is carried out on two other levels that are considered more relevant than the questions regarding the labour theory of value. One is Marx's general law of accumulation – appearing in Chapter 25 of the Moscow edition of Volume I of *Capital* (1887) – where for the first time in the history of economics a theory of cyclical unemployment is produced based on the strict inverse relation between the rate of profits and the wage rate. Using a fundamental paper by Sylos Labini (1984b), Marx's approach is compared with that of Joseph Schumpeter. It is pointed out that Marx's law depends wholly on the pure single-sector corn framework and that the problem of effective demand is excluded. The second level concerns the macroeconomic modernity of Marx's physiocratic-inspired schemes of reproduction. With Sweezy's (1942) unsurpassed book, the schemes are shown to entail structural discontinuities in production phases and the systematic emergence of the problem of realization and of disproportionalities. We also illustrate how the role assigned to the capital goods sector establishes a definite hierarchy in production, opening up new horizons on the evolution of historical industrial phases, a theme relevant for development and planning courses. The section is ended by relating Rosa Luxemburg's theoretical break arising from her novel understanding of Marx's schemes of reproduction. It is emphasized that her approach is a main component of Michal Kalecki's contribution to the theory of effective demand.

3.2   Neoclassical Economics: Marshall, Walras and Wicksell

The rise of marginalism is illustrated as a deliberate break with the classical cost of production price theory. Furthermore, students learn that marginalism in all its forms is based on methodological individualism: preference sets and perfect competition are the outcome of such a methodology. To this effect, several chapters of Yanis Varoufakis's (1998) microeconomic textbook are assigned. Their merit lies in that a critical philosophical discussion of the individualistic methodology accompanies every step of the analytical presentation. The next move is to bring in Sraffa's (1926) critique of the representative – hence single – firm of Marshallian economics. The course then tackles Walras's general equilibrium theory. From Walsh and Gram (1980), it is shown that Walras's original multi-sector model contains no accumulation. Knut Wicksell's objective was to complete it by building a long-period theory of capital and distribution based on the marginal productivity of the factors of production. To achieve that, Wicksell had to abandon the multi-sector approach in favour of a homogeneous notion of capital on which to construct the production function whose properties are shown via Pasinetti (1977, ch. 1). It is pointed out that, unlike the classics, capital is neither produced nor reproduced. The rate of interest emerges as a real price, equal to the marginal productivity of capital, which defines both the capital intensity of production and the equality between saving and investment, while savings arise out of preference for future consumption. Hence, the real rate of interest expresses also intertemporal consumption choices. At this point, students are asked to concentrate on the fact that (1) the Wicksellian production function holds only if there is one good, or if each and every good is produced by the same technique of production; and (2) saving as future consumption is possible only in a non-monetary economy like a self-sufficient farm.

3.3   The Watershed: Keynes and Kalecki

From the notion of intertemporal consumption, we move directly to Keynes's own demolition of the concept:

> [...] an act of individual saving means – so to speak – a decision not to have dinner today. But it does not necessitate a decision to have dinner or to buy a pair of boots a week hence or a year hence or to consume any specified thing at any specified date. Thus, it depresses the business of preparing today's dinner without stimulating the business of making ready for some future act of consumption. It is not a substitution of future consumption demand for present consumption demand – it is a net diminution of such demand. (Keynes, 1936, p. 210)

Conceptually the quotation is a rejection of Wicksell's and Ramsey's theory of saving, as well as a negation of Smith's phrase 'every frugal man [is] a public benefactor'. From this we proceed to illustrate Keynes's apparatus through the insightful Chapter 2 of Pasinetti's (1974) essays on growth. In it the determination of saving by investment independently from the rate of interest is lucidly spelled out. The next step consists in questioning the standard view that downward wage flexibility eliminates unemployment. We use a Kalecki classic, discussing money and real wages (Kalecki [1939] 1966). There it is proven that under the unusual case of perfect competition, a fall in money wages would lead to a fall in marginal costs and, therefore, in prices without any gain in employment. Under the more general case of imperfect competition, prices will not fall in proportion to wage cuts. Unemployment will rise due to the decline in real wages, and in wage earners' consumption. A comparison between Kalecki and Keynes follows on the basis of an illuminating paper by Peter Kriesler (1997) where Kalecki's use of Marx's schemes of reproduction is brought to the fore. Students should by now be able to grasp the break caused by Keynes and Kalecki in making investment drive saving and in showing that wage cuts increase unemployment.

4   THE POST-1945 DECADES: THE CENTRAL ROLE OF THE USA AND NEOCLASSICAL ECONOMICS

The second half of the course recoups the critique of Wicksell's capital theory, applying it to Solow's growth model. It also covers the transformation of Walras's economics into the Arrow–Debreu system of intertemporal equilibrium that acquires a remarkable importance in relation to rational expectations. It is shown that in the 'West' the teaching of economics began to follow at an increasing pace MIT's Paul Anthony Samuelson's *Economics* from the 1948 edition onward. It is pointed out that, over the years, the text's task was to incorporate into a doctrinal form all the elements that could bring Keynes's theory back to the fold and also establish the view that neoclassical micro-based economics tells an essentially true story about human agency. But, we observe, two other strands were being born. Its members worked in remote US institutions such as the Cowles Foundation at Yale and the Rand Corporation. One of these strands – the other being game theory research led by John von Neumann – was composed of people, like Gérard Debreu himself fresh from Paris, engaged in building an axiomatic theory of general competitive intertemporal equilibrium in which decisions are taken once for the whole lifetime of agents. The sole purpose of such a metaphysical exercise was to prove the existence of an overall market-clearing price vector. At this point it is reported to students that the exercise was successful: it turned out to be so perfect that it will not be seen anywhere (Hahn, 1980). Hence, we move onto the discussion of what the late Frank Hahn called low-brow theory.

4.1 MIT Keynesianism: The Low Brow

Students are asked to consider the following three-stage scheme on which the MIT ideology had been built until the rise of rational expectations and the arrival of Joseph Stiglitz's asymmetries shortly afterwards.

The first stage consisted in making Keynes into a special case of supply and demand theory through the Hicks–Modigliani IS–LM system where unemployment arises from the liquidity trap (Hicks) and/or from money wage rigidity (Modigliani). Neither case is a main cause of unemployment in Keynes. Students are directed to the History of Economic Thought website,[2] once hosted by the New School for Social Research in New York, where the IS–LM is treated in great detail. The second stage is represented by Robert Solow's growth model. Its Harrod–Domar origins are presented first by using Pasinetti's beautiful analysis of the transition from classical to Keynesian dynamics (1974, ch. 3). In this way, students also learn about the alternative Kaldorian approach. The main references for the Solow model proper are Harcourt (2006) and the History of Economic Thought website. We focus then on the ultimate result, namely that if the IS–LM model is applied in the short run, long-run steady state growth is assured according to the dynamics of relative factors' scarcity or abundance.

The last stage consists in the introduction of the Phillips curve. We distinguish between Phillips's own 1958 empirical paper in *Economica*, which indeed came close to Marx's observations on the inverse relation between variations in the wage rate and unemployment, and the policy Phillips curve jointly produced by Samuelson and Solow (1960). The MIT economic ideology ends up sounding as follows: 'We at MIT can solve everything through neoclassical supply and demand theory. Keynes is for the short run and his problem can be fixed by toggling either the fiscal policy button or the monetary policy one, or both. Once the short-run problem is addressed we will travel along Solow's full employment smooth growth path. Yet, before we take off we need to establish through the – supposedly stable – Phillips curve the trade-off between inflation and unemployment. If the President wishes to have low inflation he must accept a higher rate unemployment'. But is the Phillips curve stable? Here we move on to Milton Friedman's inflationary expectations-augmented Phillips curve. It is portrayed as an important, albeit anti-Keynesian, critique because it questioned the whole validity of the Phillips curve. It played a significant role in the revival of monetarism, which quickly turned into rational expectations.

4.2   The Crisis of the MIT Ideology

The MIT people really believed that good policy making was like pulling levers and toggling buttons. In 1971, an advanced textbook for MIT doctoral courses was published, aiming to provide a framework for monetary and fiscal policies (Foley and Sidrauski, 1971). The text was the extension of Solow's growth model to a two-sector economy formed by a capital and a consumption goods sector. The theoretical basis of the book is wrong on two accounts: the Solow model is flawed; its two-sector variant is equally so and even more absurd.

Now the Cambridge UK story is being unfolded before the students. The main paper to which they are exposed is Harcourt's

(1969) masterly account of the capital controversy and its main characters: Paul Samuelson, Pierangelo Garegnani, Luigi Pasinetti and Joan Robinson. They therefore learn that Samuelson's (1962) attempt to provide a comprehensive Wicksell–Ramsey–Clark neo-classical parable failed – as Samuelson himself admitted in a famous symposium organized by the *Quarterly Journal of Economics* in 1966 (Levhari and Samuelson, 1966) – because it was based on the impossible task of ascribing to capital a natural marginal productivity, which would then define its price as well as its rate of return. This desperate attempt to generalize the single-product Wicksellian production function led Samuelson to force everything into a special case where techniques have to be identical everywhere, like in Marx's uniform organic composition of capital. Last, the two-sector model is tackled by presenting a synthesis of a seminal essay by Luigi Spaventa (1970) where the ad hoc stability conditions required to make it behave like the Solow model are highlighted.

Students are required to metabolize the fact that neoclassical factors substitution theory is hollow. The whole issue is wrapped up in a more recent paper by Luigi Pasinetti (2000) while Harcourt (2006, ch. 7) provides a systemic alternative view of growth theory from Adam Smith to the present. The section is closed with two observations. First, the MIT ideology did not collapse because their models were wrong – the objections were ultimately ignored. The critiques, however, are still valid. Today, neoclassical econometric production functions are being widely applied although they are even worse than wrong (Felipe and McCombie, 2013). Second, and more importantly, the crisis of MIT economics was caused by the crisis within US society of a political economy based on military Keynesianism through the Vietnam War.

4.3   Rational Expectations and General Equilibrium

Chicago's rational expectations filled the vacuum left by the more than justified collapse of MIT's and Yale's macroeconomics. Students are given to read what is still the clearest and simplest explanation of rational expectations (Maddock and Carter, 1982). It is important that the theoretical reasons that led to the hegemony of Chicago economics be understood. These are explained with Modigliani's (1977) presidential address to the American Economic Association where he maintained that in the long run we will all be living in a

Walrasian perfectly competitive world since wage and price rigidities are purely short-run phenomena. If Modigliani assumes the world to be ultimately Walrasian, it stands to reason to also assume that agents, being no fools, will, from the start, make rational use of all the available information in a manner consistent with the Walrasian *Weltanschauung* (worldview) of both Chicago and MIT. For rational expectations therefore, the actual economy is in an Arrow–Debreu state with market clearing prices and full employment. The Phillips curve becomes vertical and money super-neutrality rules. It is brought to students' attention that to avoid conflicting tendencies in agents' behaviour, Lucasian economics must assume the existence of a single representative agent.

The Sorbonne University mathematician Bernard Guerrien (2004) successfully expressed in beautiful didactical terms the economic meaning of an all-important offshoot of the Arrow–Debreu theory, namely the Sonnenschein–Mantel–Debreu (SMD) results – aka the 'anything goes' theorem – where a stable equilibrium between excess demand functions and prices is not likely to be obtained. Once more, microeconomic well-behaved relations cease to be so at the aggregate level (Rizvi, 2006). The claims of rational expectations are thereby as invalid as were those of Samuelson in relation to capital theory. The representative agent's device is flawed too: Alan Kirman's (1992) wonderful piece proves that the supposed single agent represents nobody. It is pointed out that although intellectually defeated, the Lucas decade did create the conditions for a form of zombie economics in the shape of dynamic stochastic general equilibrium and efficient market hypothesis models. We then study the relevant chapters of Quiggin's (2012) most stimulating book. As of 2012, the course was ended by going back to the classics, thanks to an essay by Pasinetti (2011) where it emerges how the classical concept of saving is superior to the individualistic agent-based concept.

5   CONCLUSIONS

This was a general course where history enabled us to arrive at contemporary problems. Clearly defined heterodox departments would be needed to study and develop non-marginalist price theories (Lee, 1998) and vertically integrated processes as an alternative view

of growth theory (Pasinetti, 1981). Furthermore, there is the need
to revalue the literature on the 'traverse' (Hicks, 1965; Lowe, 1976)
because it has as its end point sectoral planning for full employment,
which is relevant for addressing the main questions related to environmental policies.

NOTES

1. The phenomenal little book on physics by Carlo Rovelli – a major theorist in
   the field – first published in Italian in 2014 and now translated into English,
   performs the remarkable feat of bringing to the reader the most up-to-date results
   without eschewing complexity, precisely because it is cast in terms of the historical
   evolution of the discipline (Rovelli, 2016).
2. Accessed 9 January 2018 at http://www.hetwebsite.net/het/thought.htm.

REFERENCES

Blanchard, O. (2000), 'Défense de la science économique', *Libération*,
   accessed 14 December 2017 at http://www.liberation.fr/tribune/2000/10/16/
   defense-de-la-science-economique_340802.
Felipe, J. and J.S.L. McCombie (2013), *The Aggregate Production Function
   and the Measurement of Technical Change: 'Not Even Wrong'*, Cheltenham,
   UK and Northampton, MA, USA: Edward Elgar Publishing.
Foley, D. and M. Sidrauski (1971), *Monetary and Fiscal Policy in a Growing
   Economy*, Boston, MA: Collier Macmillan.
Guerrien, B. (2004), *La théorie économique néoclassique. T.1. Microéconomie*,
   Paris: La découverte.
Hahn, F. (1980), 'General equilibrium theory', *Public Interest*, Special
   Edition, 123–36.
Harcourt, G.C. (1969), 'Some Cambridge controversies in the theory of
   capital', *The Journal of Economic Literature*, 7(2), 369–405.
Harcourt, G.C. (2006), *The Structure of Post Keynesian Economics*,
   Cambridge, UK: Cambridge University Press.
Harcourt, G.C. and P. Riach (1997), *A Second Edition of The General
   Theory*, London and New York: Routledge.
Hicks, J. (1965), *Capital and Growth*, Oxford: Clarendon Press.
Kalecki, M. ([1939] 1966), *Studies in the Theory of Business Cycles, 1933–
   1939*, New York: A.M. Kelley.
Keynes, J.M. (1936), *The General Theory of Employment, Interest and
   Money*, London: Macmillan.
Kirman, A.P. (1992), 'Whom or what does the representative individual
   represent?', *The Journal of Economic Perspectives*, 6(2), 117–36.
Kriesler, P. (1997), 'Keynes, Kalecki and the *General Theory*', in G.C.

Harcourt and P. Riach (1997), *A Second Edition of The General Theory*, London and New York: Routledge, pp. 300–322.

Lee, F. (1998), *Post Keynesian Price Theory*, Cambridge, UK: Cambridge University Press.

Levhari, D. and P.A. Samuelson (1966), 'The nonswitching theorem is false', *The Quarterly Journal of Economics*, **80**(4), 518–19.

Lowe, A. (1976), *The Path of Economic Growth*, New York: Cambridge University Press.

Maddock, R. and M. Carter (1982), 'A child's guide to rational expectations', *The Journal of Economic Literature*, **20**(1), 39–51.

Marx, K. (1887), *Capital, A Critique of Political Economy*, Moscow: Progress Publishers. [First English edition]

Modigliani, F. (1977), 'The monetarist controversy or, should we forsake stabilization policies?', *The American Economic Review*, **67**(2), 1–19.

Myrdal, G. (1953), *The Political Element in the Development of Economic Theory*, London: Routledge & Kegan Paul.

Pasinetti, L. (1974), *Growth and Income Distribution. Essays in Economic Theory*, Cambridge, UK: Cambridge University Press.

Pasinetti, L. (1977), *Lectures in the Theory of Production*, New York: Columbia University Press.

Pasinetti, L. (1981), *Structural Change and Economic Growth*, Cambridge, UK: Cambridge University Press.

Pasinetti, L. (2000), 'Critique of neoclassical theory of growth and distribution', *BNL Quarterly Review*, **215**, 383–431.

Pasinetti, L. (2007), *Keynes and the Cambridge Keynesians: A 'Revolution in Economics' to be Accomplished*, Cambridge, UK: Cambridge University Press.

Pasinetti, L. (2011), 'A few counter-factual hypotheses on the current economic crisis', *Cambridge Journal of Economics*, **36**, 1433–53.

Phillips, A.W. (1958), 'The relation between unemployment and the rate of change of money wage rates in the United Kingdom, 1861–1957', *Economica*, New Series, **25**(100), 283–99.

Quiggin, J. (2012), *Zombie Economics: How Dead Ideas Still Walk Among Us*, Princeton, NJ: Princeton University Press.

Ricardo, D. (1815), *An Essay on Profits*, London: John Murray.

Rizvi, S. Abu and A. Turab (2006), 'The Sonnenschein–Mantel–Debreu results after thirty years', *History of Political Economy*, **38** (annual suppl.), 228–45.

Robinson, J. (1972), 'The second crisis of economic theory', *The American Economic Review*, **62**(1/2), 1–10.

Roncaglia, A. (2005), *The Wealth of Ideas*, Cambridge, UK: Cambridge University Press. [Originally published in Italian]

Rovelli, C. (2016), *Seven Brief Lessons on Physics*, London: Penguin.

Samuelson, P.A. (1948), *Economics*, New York: McGraw-Hill.

Samuelson, P.A. (1962), 'Parable and realism in capital theory: The surrogate production function', *The Review of Economic Studies*, **29**(3), 193–206.

Samuelson, P.A. and R. Solow (1960), 'Analytical aspects of anti-inflation policy', *The American Economic Review*, **50**(2), 177–94.

Spaventa, L. (1970), 'Rate of profit, rate of growth, and capital intensity in a simple production model', *Oxford Economic Papers*, **22**(2), 129–47.

Sraffa, P. (1926), 'The laws of return under competitive conditions', *The Economic Journal*, **36**(144), 535–50.

Sraffa, P. (1960), *Production of Commodities by Means of Commodities*, Cambridge, UK: Cambridge University Press.

Sweezy, P.M. (1942), *The Theory of Capitalist Development*, Oxford: Oxford University Press.

Sylos Labini, P. (1984a), 'Competition and economics growth in Adam Smith', in *The Forces of Economics Growth and Decline*, Cambridge, MA: MIT Press, pp. 3–36.

Sylos Labini, P. (1984b), 'The problem of economic growth in Marx and Schumpeter', in *The Forces of Economics Growth and Decline*, Cambridge, MA: MIT Press, pp. 37–78.

Tarshis, L. and E. Stephenson Furniss (1947), *The Elements of Economics: An Introduction to the Theory of Price and Employment*, Boston, MA: Houghton Mifflin.

Varoufakis, Y. (1998), *Foundations of Economics*, London: Routledge.

Walsh, V. and H. Gram (1980), *Classical and Neoclassical Theories of General Equilibrium: Historical Origins and Mathematical Structure*, New York: Oxford University Press.

4. From teaching history of economic thought to teaching and learning with historical perspectives

Daniela Tavasci

1 BACKGROUND

The idea of presenting this experience of teaching and learning the history of economic thought (HET) at the School of Economics and Finance (SEF) at Queen Mary University of London (QMUL) stemmed from the first Teaching with Historical Perspectives (THP) workshop organized by the SEF, QMUL, in May 2016. A number of academics and students met to discuss their experience of teaching and learning HET and of integrating it into other subdisciplines, including microeconomics, macroeconomics and finance in very different institutions.

In 2011, I joined SEF at QMUL. My teaching load included the design of an HET module, which the students had asked for in order to make sense of the references to various schools of thought that the specialist media (e.g., the *Financial Times*, *The Economist*) were making in commenting on the recent financial crisis. I initially pursued a traditional approach to my teaching, presenting a chronological overview of significant economists across the HET. However, I soon realized that this approach had strong limitations and failed to engage the students to a great extent. Students had chosen this module because they were deeply interested, but their interest was not well served by the long sequence of economists and schools of thought presented in their textbooks. I also struggled to find a good textbook that was pitched at the right level – it seemed that there was a considerable trade-off between rigour and simplicity amongst the textbooks that I examined. I eventually opted for Roncaglia's *Wealth of Ideas* (Roncaglia, 2006), but I soon realized that most of my students were not used to abstract thinking and had studied neither history nor the history of philosophy; they were more used to mathematics and economics. As a result, I needed to support them with my teaching notes and other readings to help them make sense of their textbook.

However, I also had three specific concerns. First, students were missing out on how the history of economic thought had evolved as a result of both actual events and debates within the discipline. Second, I suspected that the chronological organization of the module, on its own, would confirm the impression that economics had evolved into a progressively more rigorous science simply as a result of economists' greater level of specialization in the various subdisciplines and thanks to the development and adoption of econometric techniques that gave economics the appearance of being a hard science. Third, and related to the previous points, student movements had expressed dissatisfaction with a mainstream economics curriculum, both in the United States (Delreal, 2011) and in the United Kingdom (Post-Crash Economics Society, 2014)[1] in particular, in light of its inadequacy to explain the global financial and economic crisis. A HET module might provide an ideal opportunity for presenting a pluralist perspective within an overarching historical one.

I shared this concern with some of my mentors, including Victoria Chick (Emeritus Professor at UCL) and Roberto Veneziani (colleague at QMUL), and decided to engage in a reflective redesign (Boud and Walker, 1998; Brookfield, 1995) of my HET module that would address the desire to increase students' participation in the delivery of a module, creating the space for innovative forms of pedagogy.

What gives particular significance to this study is that my department is not known for pluralism or heterodoxy in its economics teaching. The economics curricula are relatively standard, with core modules of quantitative methods, microeconomics and macroeconomics based on mainstream syllabuses. Further, while the pursuit of a pluralist approach to economics teaching is not actively opposed, the constraints on the current curriculum design, which reflect challenges in terms of bureaucratic processes and the gathering of broad intellectual support among colleagues, entailed that the easiest way to introduce pluralist economics teaching was through establishing space within the current teaching framework. A second-year undergraduate HET module offered a 'natural space' for the introduction of pluralistic economics. In the case of QMUL, the module was launched as a result of students' demand for pluralism, and as a way of accommodating their requests in the wake of the crisis, without the need for revolutionizing the entire curriculum.

2   REDESIGNING THE MODULE

Initially, the module was taught in traditional, chronological fashion. Starting with Adam Smith, it followed with a series of economists according to the structure of standard HET textbooks, such as those of Roncaglia (2006) and Spiegel (2002). Indeed, a chronological organization of the module was something the first cohort of students expected, and so their feedback was very positive, but the questions they posed led me to rethink the way in which the module was taught: students were confused about the fact that not all economists focused on the same questions – for example, and they were not clear about the emergence and evolution of the various schools of thought.

As a result, I decided to redesign my module. As traditional lecturing to students on the various economists had not been completely effective in this module, a deliberate attempt was made to introduce more active, collaborative learning. I therefore decided to restructure my module by following two dimensions: now the horizontal dimension follows the chronological order of traditional HET modules, starting with Adam Smith; the vertical dimension addresses certain questions that would then allow students to reflect on certain specific themes in which economics as a discipline had evolved throughout history.

A first introductory lecture presents the new structure of the module and introduces the themes of the vertical dimension. In order to avoid the one-directional dynamic between the teacher and the class, the themes are introduced simply as guidelines for reflection. They will be referred to again in the weekly discussions that concentrate on individual economists and/or schools of thoughts. In this respect then, these ideas are part of the overarching framework of the module. The opportunity for reflection comes with the weekly classes that follow the lecture. Questions are circulated at the end of each lecture and essentially guide the homework preparation for the class. A number of questions are set each week relating to the various economists and schools of thought and these represent the themes of the vertical dimension. As examples, these are often related to what constitutes the backbone of the specific system of thought – for example, the economic problem (or what economics is about), the assumptions, the methods of enquiry, the methodology, but also how individual schools of thought emerged in response to actual economic problems or as a result of debates within the disciplines, how the state is perceived, and what is the idea of the market with regard to the economy. As a result, the policy prescriptions associated with each school of thought are questioned with respect to their distributional implications. Each week then includes a specific reflection on these points.

The aims of this restructuring are various. An effort is made to refer to current issues, and this further engages students. First, they are encouraged to look at various economists in their own contexts (Heilbroner, 2000), but also, and this is most important, in relation to their *systems* of thought, rather than to a list of non-integrated points. This way of proceeding encourages critical thinking: for example, a frequent question is to address the role played in Ricardo's political view by both his theory of rent and his theory of comparative advantage. The latter theory is usually known to students: they are aware of its narrative; they are able to solve some exercises in a more or less mechanical way. However, for the first time, by the second lecture, students are exposed to the idea that the policy prescription underpinned by the theory of comparative advantage is biased towards a particular social class to the detriment of another: Ricardo was in favour of capital accumulation against the parasitic class of landlord; he tries to influence Britain's trade policy and keep food prices low even against the interests of the rural aristocracy of the time. This is a first strike against the idea that economics is a politically neutral technical apparatus. This results in greater student engagement since it makes it easier for the lecturer to find some relevance for today's political and economic integration of one country or region into the world economy: last year, a discussion about the distributional implications of Brexit naturally emerged within class debate.

Second, and to some extent this is another aspect of the first point, students become aware that progress in economics arises through debates and controversies and not merely as a result of the subject's evolving technical apparatus. Ricardo engaged in the debates about the Corn Laws and the Poor Laws. Most notably, Keynes and Hayek also argued over the role of state intervention. Today, we have similarly fierce debates about state intervention and its distributional implications.

Third, and as an immediate consequence of the previous points, there is no single economics: the module offers an exposure to pluralism defined in the widest sense. Once students are exposed to the idea of pluralism, the temptation is to ask which school of thought or economist is right. This might seem a naive approach, but it is difficult to oppose since it is shared even by established researchers. A discussion about the controversial definition of pluralism in economics is beyond the scope of this chapter. However, the approach used here is not in line with Groenewegen's definition of pluralism as 'a combination of mainstream economics with more heterodox approaches in such a way that the student is not confused, but better understands the possibilities and limitations of different schools of thought in economics' (Groenewegen, 2007, p. 14). On the contrary, here the issue is not so much to evaluate different approaches, rather it is to locate historically the approaches within various schools and see them as systems of thought generated within particular historical and intellectual contexts. As a result, the approach used in teaching economics with historical perspectives that informs my teaching is in line with an integrated approach that combines an involvement in philosophy, economic history and the history of economic thought with the idea that the evolution of economic principles does not come from nowhere, simply as a result of what new mathematical techniques allowed economists to do.

Fourth, students are asked each week to search the writings of the various economists prior to the lecture. Essentially, this is to instil distrust in received knowledge such as textbooks. A blatant example is Adam Smith and his approach to self-interest. Students are asked whether Adam Smith really believed in self-interest as the only core element of human behaviour. It is very common that students return to class surprised by their discovery of the theory of moral sentiments (Smith [1759] 2010), which leads inevitably to discussion around the relation, in his system of thought, between self-interest and sympathy. The class leader will draw attention during the class debate to the fact that this has been a sensational discovery for the students, since they had always been led to believe that Adam Smith was the economist of self-interest. This stimulates interest in what each economist really thought, as opposed to someone else's interpretation of it.

Finally, we are led to a snapshot of the present state of economics as a discipline and students are exposed to what Roncaglia refers to as 'the era of fragmentation' (Roncaglia, 2006, p. 468). The idea that economics as a discipline is fragmented into a myriad of subdisciplines resonates in the explanation of how economists were unable to anticipate the gravity and severity of the recent crisis, both in the United States and in the United Kingdom. Along similar lines, Rodrik and Eichengreen are both critical of mainstream economics, though they are not exactly heterodox economists. Eichengreen (2009) claims:

> It was not the failure or inability of economists to model conflicts of interest, incentives to take excessive risk and information problems that can give rise to bubbles, panics and crises... Rather, the problem was a partial and blinkered reading of that literature. (Eichengreen, 2009)

Rodrik (2007, p. 5) declares:

> One of the professional deformations of economists is to see an economy's problems almost exclusively from the perspective of their own area of specialty. A trade theorist will turn to developing economies and see lack of openness to trade as the key obstacle to growth. A financial market economist will identify imperfections in credit markets and lack of financial depth as the main culprit. A macroeconomist will worry about budget deficits, levels of debt, and inflation. A political-economy specialist will blame weakness in property rights and other institutions. A labor economist will point to labor-market rigidities. Each of them will then advocate a demanding set of institutional and governance reforms targeted at removing the presumed defect.

In the United Kingdom, the economists of the British Academy addressed the question asked by the Queen on why such a considerable economic turmoil was not anticipated:

> So in summary, Your Majesty, the failure to foresee the timing, extent and severity of the crisis and to head it off, while it had many causes, was principally a failure of the collective imagination of many bright people, both in this country and internationally, to understand the risks to the system as a whole. (British Academy Forum, 2009)

The module addresses this question of effectiveness of economics as a discipline in a longer-run context, discussing the initial narrowing of the economics discipline, followed by its re-expansion through the application of its technical framework to a wide range of issues (Milonakis and Fine, 2009).

With respect to teaching style, I decided to adopt a problem-based approach, which I adapted to the THP approach. As discussed in the introduction of this volume and in Chapter 8 by Luigi Ventimiglia, THP is a student-centred approach to teaching and learning closely related to the problem-based learning method. It is based on the idea that students are presented with the same problems that economists of the past faced, so that it is possible for them to retrace and interpret the solutions and the policy prescriptions that these past economists provided. Each economic theory, then, is not just a model from the textbook, it is a solution to a real problem produced by some specific economist in response to a specific real economic problem – or, increasingly frequently in more recent times, as a result of the debates within the discipline. Thus, THP presents various (historical) perspectives to the same problem and exposes students both to the evolution of the economic reality and to the corresponding evolution of the history of economic thought, as a result of both changes in the economy and debates amongst various economists and schools of thought. In this respect, then, this approach provides a context and an experience of teaching and learning in which authenticity, pluralism and, as a result, career relevance are fostered. As a consequence, THP helps students to develop the problem-solving and debating skills that are so essential for a professional economist. The assessment questions are constructively 'aligned' during the design process of the module to ensure that assessments are consistent with delivery method and content. A discussion around alignment is beyond the scope of this chapter; however, 'constructive alignment' (Biggs and Tang, 2007) is part of best practice adopted at Queen Mary University of London.

Nevertheless, after the restructuring of the module, I realized that some of these features might have been unclear to students on account of my reluctance to address too explicitly the flaws in the traditional economics teaching that was the approach generally used in the department, which was unsympathetic and sometimes hostile towards pluralism, let alone heterodox economics. I therefore decided to incorporate these into the first lecture and to provide actual present-day examples, in addition to examples from the history of economic thought, that students could familiarize themselves with and reflect on, relating them each week to specific systems of thought.

3 EVALUATING THE LEARNING AND TEACHING EXPERIENCE OF THE NEW APPROACHES

Neoclassical propositions are scrutinized and assessed in the module as are neoclassical economics' competing schools of thought. Such an approach reconstructs across a set of topics the main building blocks both of neoclassical economics and of a selection of alternative theories across the history of economic thought. An important element of this approach is to clarify the relationship between particular theories and their socio-historical context, with the aim of generating a more meaningful discussion about competing theories. To be sure, the context could be examined at greater depth, and the historical content of my module is by no means comparable to that of a module of economic history. Nevertheless, it provides a minimal historical contextualization in order to confute the idea of a single economics that has evolved over time as a result of improvements in its technical apparatus.

As a lecturer, with regard to my experience of this process of module restructuring the results have been gratifying: I have earned a number of official recognitions for the quality of my teaching. Nevertheless, I considered that my approach of using the history of economic thought as a way of exposing students to pluralism was incomplete. Often students shared this perception and commented that the module should be extended over two semesters. This dissatisfaction arose from the fact that mainstream curricula can barely scratch the surface of a treasure trove of ideas that are ignored by textbook economics, other than by encouraging independent reading and study.

Based on a research project originally developed by Deane, Van Waeyenberge and Maxwell (2016), I decided to carry out a similar approach in evaluating the module.

3.1 Methods

A mixed-methods approach was deployed, combining a short online survey with a series of semi-structured interviews. The latter were conducted with two cohorts of students who had taken the HET module in 2015/16 and in 2016/17 respectively. The anonymous online survey was designed to provide an initial overview of students' views. I decided to restrict the survey to four main questions and leave an open box for further comments. All students were invited to respond via the online learning environment. The response rate for the surveys was 38 per cent. In addition, semi-structured interviews were conducted in which themes raised in the surveys were explored. (The start-of-the-year presentation clearly addresses pluralism as one of the module's 'selling points' and as a result there is some self-selection bias, since most of the HET students are, in fact, eager to be exposed to pluralism in economics.)

3.2   Results

The survey responses shown in Table 4.1 were combined with an analysis of the data gathered through in-depth interviewing. This gave rise to the identification of a number of themes regarding the teaching and learning experience of the module.

3.2.1   Engagement and empowerment

First, the HET module played a crucial role in allowing the students to situate neoclassical economics within a spectrum of schools. From the survey, it transpired that 60 per cent of the responders were not aware that they were being taught mainly neoclassical economics in their curriculum until the start of the HET course. This was a theme that recurred throughout the interviews, with many students expressing surprise when first confronted with the reality that they had previously been studying only one particular version of economics: 'I asked my advanced micro lecturer to explain why we were taught only one side of the story, why we are taught about all these assumptions which are not used in other schools of thought' (Student 3).

While from the interviews it emerged that the awareness that neoclassical economics was not the only way to do economics caused some initial confusion (see below), this confusion generally gave way to interest, curiosity, and a sense of empowerment. Students felt they were acquiring tools to engage with economic realities that did not necessitate mastering complex mathematical skills.

The HET module is also used to escape the excessive focus on the technical apparatus of economics that the QMUL curriculum tends

Table 4.1 *Summary of answers to key questions*

Question	Before Starting University	During the First Year	At the Start of the Second Year	During the HET Module	After the HET Module Had Ended	I Am Not Aware of This
When did you first become aware that your first-year modules focused mainly on the neoclassical approaches to economics?	15% (n = 20)	15% (n = 20)	5% (n = 20)	60% (n = 20)	0	5% (n = 20)
	Yes	No				
Would you like more exposure to alternative economic theories in your economics education?	85% (n = 20)	15% (n = 20)				
	Yes	No				
Did this module help you make sense of your other economics modules?	90% (n = 20)	10% (n = 20)				
	Positive	Negative				
Do you think this module has had a positive or negative impact on your understanding of economic realities?	100% (n = 20)					

to adopt: students who are not particularly keen on quantitative elements hope to be able to improve their average grade by attending HET: 'My friends had told me that I could take this module where there was no equations but I still had to work hard and use the logic and learn a lot of stuff. Daniela has always made clear that this complements our skills. I feel that we can explain things better now and we do not need the math to do it' (Student 8).

All the students realized the importance of being exposed to pluralism in economics: 'To most of the economic questions, I have realized, the logical answer is, "it depends": for example, I have learnt that an increase in money supply might be or might not be inflationary. In actual fact, it depends on the circumstances, in terms of the theory, it depends what model and school of thought you use' (Student 5). A similar sense of revelation was achieved by inviting students to read some of the original writings of past economists: Adam Smith's theory of moral sentiments is just one example.

Sometimes, the perspective gained through the HET modules also produced distrust or disengagement with the students' standard microeconomics and macroeconomics courses.

3.2.2   Challenging and confusing

Second, students noted that they were often confused, due to their lack of initial awareness of pluralism in economics and of competing economic approaches and their sudden confrontation with a broader spectrum of the discipline. The later a student is exposed to pluralism the more confusing and challenging the experience might be. Tavasci (2017) presents serious pedagogical challenges in relation to introducing alternative economic theories into an existing mainstream curriculum, the treatment of their relationship to the existing body of neoclassical thought, the timing of introducing such theories, and the challenges that the lack of earlier exposure to a broader spectrum of economic theories entails for both lecturer and students. This subject is discussed by Repapis in Chapter 2 of this volume.

I decided to tackle this by providing an initial overarching structure that would provide students with a guide. Nevertheless, the challenge remains throughout the entire module and it is not unusual to have to return to the points of the vertical dimension along which the module is organized as a reminder to students.

3.2.3   Integration with other modules

Third, the module raised important issues regarding its relation to the rest of the curriculum. Students commented that HET remained relatively isolated from other modules and indicated their uncertainty regarding how to use the knowledge gained through HET across other modules. Their perception was that the approach in these other modules was too rigid.

Some students, on the one hand, expressed a fear of upsetting lecturers by raising what they saw as fundamental questions bearing on the relevance of what was being taught. On the other hand, they have the expectation that, throughout their studies, they will be acquiring skills that are crucial for their employability, and thus any intellectual 'digression' is likely to be considered as wasted effort.

Other students, whilst accepting that integrating HET with other standard modules can be a challenge, appreciated the attempts of lecturers to do this: a careful consideration of other modules' syllabuses led me to the reflections that eventually contributed to the adoption of THP. The approach has now been fully adopted in a couple of Finance modules and, as a result of feedback and the interviews with students, its adoption is being considered in two other modules, Games and Strategies, and Development Economics.

3.2.4   Are curriculum reforms feasible?

Fourth, a good majority of students flagged their desire for additional exposure to pluralism. During the interviews it emerged that the economics education they had received during A levels[2] and in other modules is strongly biased towards neoclassical teaching. They had received no exposure in their earlier economics education to the existence of concurrent economic theories or to how economics evolved and mainstream economics changed over time. This brings into question the way in which economics is taught, and this in turn, as discussed by Rochon and Rossi in Chapter 7 of this volume, affects how policy prescriptions and regulation are designed.

The continuing introduction of THP at QMUL may provide further opportunities for trying to overcome some of this confusion. The project remains very challenging, however, and suffers from the drawback that HET has to rely on limited space and time, with the duration of the course limited to a single semester. As a result, the historical perspectives are often restricted to little more than a mere timeline. Nevertheless, THP gives students a sense of the evolving nature of economics as a discipline as opposed to the rigid scaffolding of its technical and mathematical apparatus.

3.2.5 Employability

Fifth (a point that has been raised by other colleagues within the department who have adopted the THP approach), THP has to be seen in connection with the commodification of higher education (Molesworth, Scullion and Nixon, 2011). With the high level of fees and student indebtedness, students are always concerned that, whilst HET provides them with an interesting insight into economics and increases their intellectual awareness, the THP approach within HET and other modules may not enhance their employability skills.

For this reason, I decided to tackle this argument upfront and included in the syllabus of the module, as an intended learning outcome, the promise that it would provide critical thinking skills by exposing students to various and competing economic theories. I also added that these skills were invaluable and positively unexpected since prospective employers were already aware of QMUL students' command of technical skills. This discredits a common argument that is often deployed against the introduction of alternative approaches, namely the suggestion that students need to focus on core micro- and macro-theory as these offer a skill set that prospective employers are looking for.

Our research illustrates that students are aware that the development of critical thinking skills is important for future employment prospects and that these skills are fostered through both the teaching approach and the theoretical content of this course.

3.3 Teaching Approach

The final component of the research project sought an evaluation of the pedagogical approach adopted in the revised module. Students who completed the survey indicated that the introduction of different teaching methods was an engaging feature of the module.

The analysis of students' feedback has led to discussion both amongst staff within the School of Economics and Finance and more widely. The result has been the proposal to adopt more widely the various methods of teaching economics pioneered in the THP approach described above. As well as the continuous interaction with students, two elements have been pivotal at QMUL in designing this new teaching approach. One has been the exposure to pedagogical debates, thanks to the QMUL learning institute, now the Centre for Professional Development (CPD), which helped in refining the problem-based approach and in adapting it to THP. The second element has been the discussion with academics from other disciplines, both within QMUL and more broadly, which has exposed us to similar discussions about the history of disciplines and whether and how these can be incorporated into the curriculum.

The findings provide evidence of student interest in the introduction of alternative economic theories, further demonstrated by the fact that they deliberately signed up for such an approach, since the module description is very clear about this. They also illustrate that once exposed to alternative theories, students respond eagerly. This contradicts the commonly advanced argument that there is no student appetite for the introduction of alternative theories.

4   CONCLUSION

This chapter has reported on an attempt to bring pluralism into undergraduate economics education in a notably mainstream institution, the School of Economics and Finance of Queen Mary University of London. A new HET module was introduced with the intention of bringing more pluralism into the curriculum in a controlled manner, confined within one module and non-disruptive with respect to the other modules, and as a response to an explicit and strong demand from students.

All the students who participated in the small research survey indicated that they were keen to acquire a better understanding of various economic debates, even those who had indicated initial confusion when confronted with a broader spectrum of economic theories.

The module underwent a restructuring, with a shift towards a more student-led teaching and learning experience, and this seems to have been successful in generating a new skill set in terms of critical thinking, perhaps even improving prospects for employability.

The research has enabled me to challenge a number of myths regarding the desire, feasibility and employability concerns that tend to be used as arguments against the introduction of alternative perspectives in economics education. Students reacted positively to the efforts of lecturers to broaden their economics education. Often they expressed a desire for more such efforts as well as for these to be introduced at an earlier stage in the curriculum.

NOTES

1. See http://www.post-crasheconomics.com/about_us/, accessed 14 December 2017.
2. Equivalent to the high school diploma in the United States.

REFERENCES

Biggs, J. and C. Tang (2007), *Teaching for Quality Learning at University*, 4th edition, Buckingham: Open University Press.

Boud, D. and D. Walker (1998), 'Promoting reflection in professional courses: The challenge of context', *Studies in Higher Education*, **23**(2), 191–206.

British Academy Forum (2009), 'Letter from Professors Tim Besley and Peter Hennessy to Her Majesty the Queen', 22 July, accessed 18 July 2017 at http://wwwf.imperial.ac.uk/~bin06/M3A22/queen-lse.pdf.

Brookfield, S. (1995), *Becoming a Critically Reflective Teacher*, San Francisco, CA: Jossey-Bass.

Deane, K.E., E. Van Waeyenberge and R. Maxwell (2018), 'Recharting the history of economic thought: Approaches to and student experiences of the introduction of pluralist teaching in an undergraduate economics curriculum', forthcoming in the *International Journal for Pluralism in Economics Education*, **1**, pp. 5–34.

Delreal, J.A. (2011), 'Students walk out of Ec 10 in solidarity with "Occupy"', *The Harvard Crimson*, 2 November, accessed 18 July 2017 at http://www.thecrimson.com/article/2011/11/2/mankiw-walkout-economics-10/.

Eichengreen, B. (2009), 'The future of macro: Barry Eichengreen's take', *Bradford-Delong.com*, accessed 14 December 2017 at http://www.bradford-delong.com/2009/09/the-future-of-macro-barry-eichengreens-take.html.

Groenewegen, J. (2007), *Teaching Pluralism in Economics*, Cheltenham, UK and Northampton, MA, USA: Edward Elgar Publishing.

Heilbroner, R.L. (2000), *The Worldly Philosophers: The Lives, Times, and Ideas of the Great Economic Thinkers*, revised 7th edition, London: Penguin.

Milonakis, D. and B. Fine (2009), *From Political Economy to Economics: Method, the Social and the Historical in the Evolution of Economic Theory*, Abingdon: Routledge.

Molesworth, M., R. Scullion and E. Nixon (2011), *The Marketisation of Higher Education and the Student as Consumer*, London and New York: Routledge.

Post-Crash Economics Society (2014), *Economics, Education and Unlearning: Economics Education at the University of Manchester*, Manchester: Post-Crash Economics Society.

Rodrik, D. (2007), *One Economics, Many Recipes: Globalization, Institutions and Economic Growth*, Princeton, NJ: Princeton University Press.

Roncaglia, A. (2006), *The Wealth of Ideas*, Cambridge, UK: Cambridge University Press.

Smith, A. ([1759] 2010), *The Theory of Moral Sentiments*, accessed 14 December 2017 at www.earlymoderntexts.com/assets/pdfs/smith1759.pdf.

Spiegel, H.W. (2002), *The Growth of Economic Thought*, Durham, NC: Duke University Press.

Tavasci, D. (2017), 'Teaching with historical perspectives: The case of development economics', in C. Morelli and O. Feraboli (eds), *Post Crash Economics: Heterodox and Pluralist Ideas in Teaching and Research*, London: Palgrave Macmillan, 173–195.

5. Eleven theses on political economy and 'rethinking economics': The role of the history of economic thought in the 'Italian tradition'

Riccardo Bellofiore

1 INTRODUCTION

The 'theses' published here were written for the first time 15 years ago, then rewritten more than a decade ago as an intervention in a roundtable. Some updating has been done for the present publication. They have had a long gestation; in fact, the maturation of the theses covers my entire life in academia, first as a student and then as a teacher.

I began studying economic theory, but I was enrolled in a Law faculty – my interest in (the critique of) political economy, in 1973–74, grew for political reasons, and because I was lucky enough to follow an incredibly inspiring course by Claudio Napoleoni at the University of Turin (the faculty was Political Sciences) on the Italian economy from 1945 to the present, in which he discussed the many theoretical interpretations of the various theories (classical, neoclassical, Keynesian, neo-Ricardian, Marxian), and provided the foundations for understanding them. A similar approach was taken in the book by Mariano D'Antonio (*Sviluppo e crisi del capitalismo italiano 1951–1972*, De Donato, 1973), which was adopted as a textbook. Actually, my courses have always tried to replicate that same method, which I encountered again in Augusto Graziani – a method according to which there is no separation between learning about the theories of the past and *doing* economic theory today.

The issues of how to teach economic theory and its relation with the history of economic thought were implicit in the discussion about 'the second crisis of economic theory'. I limit myself to recalling the importance in those years of the Richard T. Ely Lecture by Joan Robinson published in the *American Economic Journal* (Nos. 1–2, 1972) with that very title; and an article by Suzanne de Brunhoff with Michel Beaud and Claude Servolin in *Le Monde* on 'La crise de la science économique' (22 May 1973). In those early years of my university studies at least three books were published dealing with the declared crisis of economic theory: *The Self-criticism of the Economist* (*L'autocritica dell'economista*, edited by Federico Caffè, published by Laterza, 1975), *The Crisis of Economic Theories after the Heyday of Keynesianism* (*La crisi post-keynesiana*, edited by Mariano D'Antonio, published by Boringhieri, 1975) and *The Crisis in Economic Theory* (edited by Daniel Bell and Irving Kristol, published by Basic Books, 1981 and translated into Italian as *La crisi della teoria economica* and published by Edizioni di Comunità, 1982). The debate was conducted also, if not mainly, in theoretical-political journals – particularly important was a double issue of the influential journal *Problemi del socialismo* and a debate on Marx and/versus Sraffa published in *Rinascita*, the weekly magazine of the Communist Party. The two debates went on in 1973–74 and were, in fact, one, since both were concerned with the same question – namely, how to teach economic theory and what was the meaning of critical economic theory.

At the time, the point was not just an appeal for pluralism, but the practice of plurality, with conflict among different styles of economic thinking, and fierce discussions within 'heterodoxy' itself. After the U-turn in economic theory that marked the end of the 1970s and the normalization of the teaching of economics already accomplished in the early 1980s, the debate about a crisis in economics was reopened in a letter to the daily newspaper *La Repubblica* from important Italian economists of different orientations: Giacomo Becattini, Onorato Castellino, Orlando D'Alauro, Giorgio Fuà, Siro Lombardini, Sergio Ricossa, Paolo Sylos Labini (*Lettera al Direttore*, 30 September 1988). They lamented the excesses of formalization and the abandonment of relevance in economic studies. The letter was followed the next year by two conferences organized by Stefano Zamagni and Augusto Graziani, which led to a collection of papers edited by Giacomo Becattini (*Economisti allo specchio*, Vallecchi, 1991). I intervened with a letter to the newspaper *il manifesto*, an article in the journal *Politica ed Economia*, and a review of Becattini's book in the monthly magazine *L'Indice dei libri del mese*.

My position is the one represented in the theses, and has not changed much – I think that the criticism of abstraction and formalization, and the demand for pluralism, are understandable but weak. The point is not a safe space for heterodoxy, which will never be conceded and does not mean much: it is to develop heretical economic thinking that has the ambition of becoming the general theory and of displacing orthodoxy and reducing it to a partial theory (as Marx did with Ricardo, Schumpeter with Walras, Keynes with Marshall). My convictions matured also as a result of an international round of students' protests against the way economics was taught. These began in France in 2000 as the Mouvement des étudiants pour la réforme de l'enseignement de l'économie, which then became known as the Post-Autistic Economics Movement or as a 'plea for a real-world economics'. I discussed the issue raised by the movement with Joseph Halevi in 2001 in the magazine *La rivista del manifesto*, where we agreed on everything except Marx (though I am not sure we differ too much even there, except in our rhetoric).

The immediate occasion to write the theses was an intervention at a 2001 meeting at which the Society of the History of Economic Thought was split in two. Some in the original society, AISPE (Associazione Italiana per la Storia del Pensiero Economico), wanted the focus to be strictly on the history of economic thought in its narrowest definition, without seeing that it was integral to economic theorizing. A new society was then created, STOREP (Associazione Italiana per la Storia dell'Economia Politica), which consisted mainly of political economists practising the history of economic thought. I thought that rather than just sanctioning this split within the corridors of academia, what was needed was to raise the discussion to the level of principles, and prepared a short oral intervention. I presented my theses again in 2006, in a debate with the younger generation about the future of the history of economic thought: the title of the session was 'La storia del pensiero economico italiano e le giovani generazioni' (The history of economic thought and the younger generation). I circulated it again, with a few changes, as a reaction to the Rethinking Economics movement.

The bibliography at the end of this chapter is very partial, providing just a small sample of books (no more than four for each author) by economists belonging to what I call in the theses the 'Italian tradition'. I have listed the English edition if available. The choice is, of course, personal.

2   THE 11 THESES

1. The capitalist economy is again in a profound systemic and structural crisis. This fact has been followed by a plea for more 'pluralism' in the teaching of economics. Among the protagonists of this request have been the students demanding that economics be 'rethought'. I think that a useful point of departure to discuss this situation could be the role of the history of economic thought in the curricula of the faculties where economics is taught, woven together with what I propose to call the peculiar 1950s–1980s' 'Italian tradition' in political economy. Rethinking economics could very much profit from the Italian tradition, but the latter is moribund in Italy itself because of the accelerated normalization of the Italian university.

2. My starting point is this: there exists a specificity – a distinctive and positive peculiarity – of the role that the history of economic thought has played in Italy since the 1950s (probably the first example of this, according to Augusto Graziani, was Claudio Napoleoni's *Dizionario di economia politica*, Edizioni di Comunità, 1956). This specificity informed Italian economic thinking in the 1960s and the 1970s, but has been attacked since the early 1980s' U-turn in economic theory and economic policy. Today we are witnessing the final phase of an ethnic cleansing against that tradition. The peculiarity I am talking about can be defined in the following way: no clear-cut distinction was made between the positive construction of 'knowledge' in economic theory and policy on the one hand and the history of economic thought on the other, with the two often overlapping – that amalgamation between economic theory and the history of economic thought was essential to the 'research' producing that knowledge, and to the 'teaching' accompanying research and knowledge.

3. The names of the best representatives of the Italian tradition are well known: Augusto Graziani, Claudio Napoleoni, Paolo Sylos Labini, Marcello de Cecco, Luigi Lodovico Pasinetti, Pierangelo Garegnani, Fernando Vianello, Federico Caffè,

Giacomo Becattini, Siro Lombardini, and others. The 'state of the art' of economic theory was assessed in a peculiar way by the most important economists of the Italian tradition I am referring to. Economic theory was thought of as a discipline crossed by the contemporary existence of alternative 'styles of scientific thinking' (or paradigms, to use a more standard terminology): they were not only different but in conflict, both in their fundamental theoretical grounds and in their analytical results. Most of the authors thought that each of the conflicting approaches had unresolved internal difficulties: there was a division on the issue if this problematic status of economic theory could be solved within the received knowledge. This historical-analytical evaluation of competing theories was taken to be preliminary to any advance on the contested terrains among the different approaches: value/distribution, money/inflation, reproduction/crisis.

4. The intermingling of research into the history of economic thought and the proposition of novel perspectives in economic analysis has for decades saved most of the Italian economists from the twin evils of unoriginal subalternity to the mainstream and heterodox sectarianism. On the other hand, it has been instrumental in another peculiarity of the Italian tradition: a close interdependence between controversies on theoretical issues and economic policy interventions. This second trait was a safeguard against another pair of evils: excessive simplification and theorizing divorced from reality.

5. If one stays close to this starting point and this Italian tradition, one should coherently reject, or find less interesting, other possible definitions of the history of economic thought. I just give a quick list of some alternatives: (i) history of economic thought as the history of the continuous expulsion of errors and glorious processual construction of the unique (neoclassical) Truth; (ii) history of economic thought as a mere chronological sequence of unrelated economic doctrines, the history of which is irrelevant for the theoretical and applied practice of the economists; (iii) history of economic thought as a preparatory study to justify the adoption in the present of some eclectic sum of positions derived from mutually incompatible conceptualizations. On the contrary, the Italian tradition was constructed on the principle that every history is contemporary history; that,

as a consequence, the history of economic thought is not only useful, but it is unique and irreplaceable in the 'construction' of both economic knowledge and economists, because the inner problematicity of the theoretical status of economic 'science' requires a deep investigation of the basic categories that should account for the discussions of the past.

6. The understanding of the history of economic thought I have put forward has sometimes been defined as the 'history of economic analysis', since this was the way Schumpeter approached the authors of the past (we find a similar method in Karl Marx's *Theories of Surplus Value* and Eugen von Böhm-Bawerk's *Capital and Interest*, or even in Keynes, or in the lectures on theories of values and distribution Sraffa held in Cambridge in the late 1920s). In the Italian tradition, an access to the history of economic thought of this kind was intended as indispensable and integral not only to research but also to the 'formation' of the economist. It was a constituent part of the teaching of the basic building blocks of the study in the first years of university courses (macroeconomics, theories of prices and distribution, economic policy). It was also required in the formulation of the hypotheses, and in the derivation of their implications, for the 'applied' enquiries in such topics as economic development, international economics, monetary economics, industrial economics, and so on.

7. A criticism may be levelled against this 'historical' approach to economic theory and this 'theoretical' approach to the history of economic thought – that it only allows for a 'backward' reading of the authors of the past. The complaint is that in this way the interpretation of the authors of the past is arbitrary. I think that this risk can be avoided. The history of economic analysis cannot be separated from a rich and faithful reconstruction of the context, the method, the language of the different theories and authors. On the one hand, privileging the mainstream's language and assessment of what is economic theory must be avoided, as if there were only one method, which is imperial- istically designed to colonize the social sciences (see Ben Fine, 1993, 'A question of economics: is it colonizing the social sci- ences?', *Economy and Society*, **28**(3), 403–25). The emphasis in the 'history of economic analysis' perspective I am maintaining here is on the plurality of the styles of economic thinking and

on the non-linearity of the development of economic thought. On the other hand, the history of economic analysis must be accompanied by other complementary approaches: the history of culture and ideas, the reading of primary sources, the critique of the texts, the perusal of the archives, and so on.

8. The Italian tradition – its way of doing economic theory through the history of economic thought, and the history of economic thought through economic theory – has entered into a phase of decline, then crisis, eventually regression, since the 1980s. We are now beyond the point of no return, at least in Italy. The crisis comes from the inside and from the outside. From the inside, among the historians of economic thought in the strict sense, the interest in 'documents' and 'archives' risks becoming overwhelming. From the outside, a series of university reforms has reduced the economic policy content of the courses in favour of a business/accountancy culture and metric, designed to appeal to students wishing to escape the supposed unrealism of economics faculties. This is a trap: what is at issue should not be abstraction as such, but the kind of abstraction that hinders the understanding of the world we live in (namely, an evolving capitalist monetary production economy). Nor is a request for pluralism enough. Pluralism should be the ethical requirement of allowing students to access the plurality of views. But I think that 'heretics' should have a bolder attitude. Keynes's principle of effective demand was presented as a more 'general theory' than Marshall's. Schumpeter proposed his theory of economic development as more general and relevant than Walras's economic logic designed for the circular flow. Marx's theory of the form of value and of the abstraction of labour turned the meaning of Ricardo's labour theory of value upside down, transforming it into a macro-monetary theory of capitalist production and exploitation. All these authors proposed a 'revolution' in economic theory – uprooting real analysis and upholding monetary analysis, to use Schumpeter's dichotomy – so that they were candidates for a new orthodoxy. They were heretics, rather than heterodox, exactly because they defined themselves positively (as founders of new approaches), rather than negatively (as internal dissenters).

9. Taking this line, the first duty in teaching economic theory against the background of a historical sensibility is to educate

students in a critical thinking that is grounded on the plurality of the visions and models that are in conflict. The conflict of ideas alludes to deeper antagonisms. This of course is exactly the reason why this style of thinking has been dropped by universities, and the last remnants of it are under attack. Nowadays in Italy the history of economic thought is marginalized in economics degrees at all levels: undergraduate, postgraduate, even doctoral studies – only a few marginal courses have survived, in either Master's or PhD programmes. In fact, their presence is a measure of the residual academic power of the individual teachers. These courses will die with the retirement of those professors.

10. The vanishing distinctiveness of the Italian economics profession, the loss of prestige of the history of economic thought, the relentless marginalization of heretics and of the historian of economic thoughts, are all phenomena that go together, though they are not identical. This commonality of destiny explains why the history of economic thought has been expelled from the essential basic requirements for becoming an economist. It is no longer a knowledge transmitted to the new generations as indispensable for orientating oneself in the dilemmatic situation of economic (and social) theory. The strategy of many heterodox economists of finding refuge in associations and journals of the history of economic thought is understandable but short-sighted. It is true that the history of economic thought is still more open to pluralism than other 'specializations' in economics. But it is a kind of Indian reservation, whose relative tranquillity is paid for with higher irrelevance in economics departments and in the teaching of economics to undergraduates, not to speak of the selection of economists.

11. If my diagnosis of the situation is correct, what is urgent is a radical turnaround. It is important that economic theory should be practised with a sensibility of how the concepts and problems have been born and how they have evolved; but it is also important that the history of economic thought is practised in such a way as to give a central role to the problematic status of economic theory today. Borrowing an expression from Joan Robinson, we are experiencing a 'third crisis of economic theory'. The turnaround I am advocating must implicate not only 'research' – a 'rethinking' of economic theory. It must

extend to the 'teaching' of economic theory and economic policy, and it must affect the 'selection' of academic economists. A thorough knowledge of the competing approaches, in their diversity, must be a compulsory requirement for becoming a professor of economics. The historical dimension of categories, the plurality of the styles of economic thinking, and the problematic status of contemporary mainstream(s), need to be part of the basic teaching from the first undergraduate course to the Master's and PhD programmes – if not, economics achieves a scientific ranking lower than astrology.

BIBLIOGRAPHY

Becattini, G. (1962), *Il concetto di industria e la teoria del valore*, Torino: Boringhieri.

Becattini, G. (1979), *Scienza economica e trasformazioni sociali*, Florence: La Nuova Italia.

Becattini, G. (2004), *Industrial Districts: A New Approach to Industrial Change*, Cheltenham, UK and Northampton, MA, USA: Edward Elgar Publishing.

Caffè, F. (1956), *Saggi sulla moderna 'economia del benessere'*, Torino: Boringhieri.

Caffè, F. (1966, 1970), *Politica economica*, 2 vols, Torino: Boringhieri.

Caffè, F. (1977), *Economia senza profeti: Contributi di bibliografia economica*, Rome: Edizioni Studium.

Caffè, F. (1981), *L'economia contemporanea: I protagonisti e altri saggi*, Rome: Edizioni Studium.

De Cecco, M. (1968), *Saggi di politica monetaria*, Milan: Giuffrè.

De Cecco, M. (1974), *Money and Empire: The International Gold Standard, 1890–1914*, Totowa, NJ: Rowman & Littlefield [Italian 1st edition, Laterza, 1969; Italian 2nd edition, Einaudi, 1979].

De Cecco, M. (1993), *L'Italia e il sistema finanziario internazionale, 1919–1936*, Bari: Laterza.

De Cecco, M. (2013), *Ma cos'è questa crisi? L'Italia, l'Europa e la seconda globalizzazione (2007–2013)*, Rome: Donzelli.

Garegnani, L. (1960), *Il capitale nelle teorie della distribuzione*, Milan: Giuffrè.

Garegnani, L. ([1962] 2015), 'Il problema della domanda effettiva nello sviluppo economico italiano', *Review of Political Economy*, **27**(2) ['On the factors that determine the volume of investment', English translation of Chapters III and IV in Garegnani, 1962].

Garegnani, L. (1979), *Valore e domanda effettiva: Keynes, la ripresa dell'economia classica e la critica ai marginalisti*, Torino: Einaudi [Cf. Garegnani's (1978) 'Notes on consumption, investment and effective

74   *Teaching the history of economic thought*

demand: I', *Cambridge Journal of Economics*, **2**(4), 335–53 and (1979) 'Notes on consumption, investment and effective demand: II', *Cambridge Journal of Economics*, **3**(1), 63–82. The 'Notes' were published in Italian in *Economia internazionale* in 1964. See also Garegnani (1976), 'On a change in the notion of equilibrium in recent work on value and distribution: A comment on Samuelson', in M. Brown, K. Sato and P. Zarembka (eds), *Essays in Modern Capital Theory*, Amsterdam: North Holland, 25–45].

Garegnani, L. (1981), *Marx e gli economisti classici*, Torino: Einaudi ['Value and distribution in the classical economists and Marx' (1984), *Oxford Economic Papers*, **36**(2), 291–325].

Graziani, A. (1976), *Teoria economica: Prezzi e distribuzione*, Naples: ESI.

Graziani, A. (1981), *Teoria Economica: Macroeconomia*, Naples: ESI.

Graziani, A. (2000), *Lo sviluppo dell'economia italiana: Dalla ricostruzione all'economia europea*, Torino: Bollati Boringhieri.

Graziani, A. (2003), *The Monetary Theory of Production*, Cambridge, UK: Cambridge University Press.

Lombardini, S. (1953), *Il monopolio nella teoria economica*, Milan: Vita e pensiero.

Lombardini, S. (1956), *L'analisi della domanda nella teoria economica*, Milan: Giuffrè.

Lombardini, S. (1985–86), *Il nuovo corso di economia politica*, 2 vols, Torino: UTET.

Napoleoni, C. (1956), *Dizionario di economia politica*, Milan: Edizioni di Comunità.

Napoleoni, C. (1968), *Economic Thought of the Twentieth Century*, London: Martin Robertson [Italian 1st edition, ERI, 1961; Italian 2nd edition, Einaudi, 1963].

Napoleoni, C. (1973), *Smith, Ricardo, Marx*, Italian 2nd edition, Turin: Boringhieri [English translation, *Smith, Ricardo, Marx: Observations on the History of Economic Thought*, Oxford: Blackwell, 1975].

Napoleoni, C. (1976), *Valore*, Milan: Isedi.

Pasinetti, L.L. (1974), *Growth and Income Distribution: Essays in Economic Theory*, Cambridge, UK: Cambridge University Press.

Pasinetti, L.L. (1977), *Lectures on the Theory of Production*, London: Macmillan.

Pasinetti, L.L. (1993), *Structural Economic Dynamics: A Theory of the Economic Consequences of Human Learning*, Cambridge, UK: Cambridge University Press.

Pasinetti, L.L. (2007), *Keynes and the Cambridge Keynesians: A 'Revolution in Economics' to be Accomplished*, Cambridge, UK: Cambridge University Press.

Sylos Labini, P. (1962), *Oligopoly and Technical Progress*, Cambridge, MA: Harvard University Press [2nd edition, 1969; Italian 1st edition, Giuffrè, 1957; Italian 3rd edition, Einaudi, 1964].

Sylos Labini, P. (1970), *Problemi dello sviluppo economico*, Bari: Laterza.

Sylos Labini, P. (1972), *Sindacati, inflazione e produttività*, Bari: Laterza.

Sylos Labini, P. (1984), *The Forces of Economic Growth and Decline*, Cambridge, MA: MIT Press.

6. Introducing institutional microeconomics through the study of the history of economic thought

Gerald Friedman

1 IT IS NOT IN THE NATURE OF TEXTBOOKS TO RECOGNIZE CONTROVERSY

Textbooks present settled science, the triumph of good ideas over bad ones, and of even better concepts over earlier inspirations. That is why they relegate history of thought to, at most, an optional chapter, an appendix, or even to some footnotes. Why devote valuable space to discussing discarded notions? Better to quarantine them in a ghetto for those curious about the origins of the true science but where they will not distract the mass of students. In a settled science, there is no reason to teach of the history of thought. As one prominent economist once said to me, it is the history of bad doctrine.

Of course, those who dispute the orthodoxy will find historical analysis helpful in developing their approach, and the history of thought has always been popular among dissidents and others who object to the dominant paradigm. Nonconformists can search through past debates to uncover the reasons for the triumph of error and the rejection of their preferred ideas. But even those who accept the current orthodoxy should regret this casual dismissal of the history of thought. As John Stuart Mill famously argued, even the worst error may advance an opposing truth because disputation, even with complete error, helps advocates of the truth to better understand their own doctrine. Through debate, advocates discover valuable nuances, views overlooked by the evolving canon. By forcing advocates to defend their truth, debate compels them to articulate their arguments more clearly. And confronting error may also serve a valuable educational function. By exposing students to alternative viewpoints, debate can lead them to a better understanding of the underlying disputes and, thus, understand better the real nature of their preferred doctrine. As Mill said of advocates who accept a doctrine as truth without considering other views:

> Their conclusion may be true, but it might be false for anything they know: they have never thrown themselves into the mental position of those who think differently from them, and considered what such persons may have to say; and consequently, they do not, in any proper sense of the word, know the doctrine that they themselves profess. They do not know those parts of it that explain and justify the remainder; the considerations that show that a fact that seemingly conflicts with another is reconcilable with it, or that, of two apparently strong reasons, one and not the other ought to be preferred. All that part of the truth that turns the scale, and decides the judgment of a completely informed mind, they are strangers to; nor is it ever really known, but to those who have attended equally and impartially to both sides, and endeavored to see the reasons of both in the strongest light. So essential is this discipline to a real understanding of moral and human subjects, that if opponents of all important truths do not exist, it is indispensable to imagine them, and supply them with the strongest arguments which the most skillful devil's advocate can conjure up. (Mill, 1978, pp. 69–70)

In what follows, I present ideas on using history of thought to illuminate economic theory in the teaching of introductory economics. In this, I draw on my experience as a life-long observer of economics teaching and from 35 years teaching introductory microeconomics, first at Tufts University and then at the University of Massachusetts at Amherst. I suggest how the study of history of thought can enhance learning both for those who follow the dominant orthodoxy and those who criticize it. Furthermore, as pedagogy, teaching history of thought can help students learn, by maintaining interest and by giving them a deeper and richer understanding of economic theory.

2   HISTORY OF THOUGHT HOLDS AN AUDIENCE

To begin: history of thought helps students learn because it welcomes them to economic theory as a matter of people trying to understand real social questions rather than pure abstraction. Economists and theorists relate well to abstract ideas but this is often poor preparation for teaching introductory economics. To be blunt: it matters little how brilliant our lectures are if no one stays awake, and the threat of an exam or a poor grade is a poor pedagogical substitute for genuine interest in the material. This is especially a problem in the large classes of new students where introductory economics is often taught. While it is possible to engage students directly and establish personal connections in small classes of veteran students, this is not possible for many of us teaching introductory courses in large and impersonal lectures, such as my 775-student lecture in introductory microeconomics. The impersonal nature of theoretical course material can be deadly in these impersonal settings. As a social science, economics is inherently abstract; we teach a theory about human behavior that is necessarily removed from the actions of any particular human being; unlike history, literature, or some social sciences like anthropology, our material does not lend itself to names and stories. Our course content, an abstract theory of behavior, is as far removed from our students' personal experience as our large lectures are from their secondary school classes. This makes it especially urgent that we find ways to introduce debate and people into our teaching.

While it is a challenge to hold the attention of students who are all the time wondering how what we are saying matters to *them*, not to mention whether their phone is more interesting, the history of economic thought provides precisely the type of content we need to attract and hold interest. Lecturing to large numbers of students is like attracting an audience to a book: we need something to hook them in and make our abstract reasoning real to them. I received advice on this subject from one of my advisers, the late economist and historian David Landes (1924–2013), after I defended my dissertation in 1985. He advised me that in writing I should refer whenever possible to specific people, call them by name, and tell their stories because that is how we help our readers connect with our material. People, he suggested, relate to people; and to hold an audience we need to show people that their content and ideas matter to people with whom they can connect. This applies as much to our teaching as to our writing. The first step in teaching is to keep the students awake and engaged; telling them stories about the *people* who developed economic theories, the real human problems that engaged them, and how their theories resolved these concerns not only teaches the theory but, more important, teaches students that they have a reason to want to learn the theory. Stories, people, and debate make economic theory come alive.

I teach microeconomics as an ongoing story of economists arguing about the basic material problems of daily life and of the organization of society to promote constructive behavior (this is the content of my somewhat unusual textbook, Friedman, 2015). I begin by discussing the basic controversies in social theory over whether there is a natural goodness in the world, whether there is a tendency towards spontaneous social harmony, whether we need social institutions to create a moral social order or whether such institutions interfere with a benign, natural order. Thus, I begin by discussing the breakup of the medieval church, and the debate carried on in the writings of Thomas Hobbes and Gottfried Leibniz over whether the world would be naturally fair without government, whether people will spontaneously cooperate or whether we need social institutions, even an oppressive government, to establish any form of justice.

I then introduce Adam Smith who wrote in the shadow of the English conquest of Scotland and continued Scottish resistance. All too well aware of the dangers of war, of how 'the pride of man makes him love to domineer,' Smith saw market competition as a way to redirect human competition and greed away from war towards competition for wealth and production for use (Smith, 1776, p. 81). Of course, these latter are not necessarily equivalent; and this gives an opportunity to discuss the social circumstances where competition for wealth leads to a search for efficient ways to produce for use, as against thievery or development of monopoly. Smith for his part, is aware of the problem. Warning that a landlord or an employer is always seeking to establish a monopoly, 'nothing mortifies him so much as to be obliged to condescend to persuade his inferiors,' Smith proposes commodity exchange and markets not only as a way of increasing output, but also as a way of constructing and maintaining a peaceful and democratic society (Smith, 1776, p. 393; also see Hirschman, 1977). Open competition forces employers to behave constructively and this is why a fair market economy requires a state strong enough, and independent enough of domination by landlords and employers, to maintain fair competition and to restrain monopoly. This is more than economics; this is social theory addressing the fundamental problems of human society.

Smith is crucial because his economic theory set the terms of all later debate in economics. I discuss his project as a work of moral philosophy seeking to guide conflicting self-interest to the welfare of all; economics concerns the material world and the production process only as a step towards the real issues that matter: the construction of a peaceful, just, and good society. This was Smith's concern, and he discussed exchange, markets, and production because he cared about larger questions of promoting human happiness through honest communities and peaceful behavior. Using Smith, I introduce the basic techniques of microeconomics as a study of individual choice within a society: the division of labor, social sympathy, the exchange of commodities through a market and price determination through supply and demand. Before moving to the neoclassical model, however, I discuss two of Smith's most famous followers, the classical economists Ricardo and Marx. These developed economics as a 'dismal science' leading to immiseration and revolution. I discuss how their concerns differed from those of Smith's 'neoclassical' followers because they separated supply and demand from price determination. For the classicists, prices are set by the cost of production subject to constant returns to scale and independent of demand. Prices and income distribution are not set by supply and demand but by social and political processes without regard for individuals and their wishes or preferences. Economics for the classicists is the study of social determination of income, and of change coming from the evolution of the forces and the relations of production.

Thus, from the study of the history of ideas, we arrive at the central concerns of the course and of economics in general: the relative importance of supply and demand or of political conflict in the determination of relative prices and the distribution of income, and whether a market economy produces the optimal mix of outputs and encourages efficient production.

3   THE HISTORY OF THOUGHT REVEALS THE CONTROVERSIES THAT MAKE ECONOMICS EXCITING

History of thought allows me to tell my students stories about people, about economists and other social thinkers, trying to solve social problems. By showing the political controversy behind economic theory, it invites students to study economics to address current social problems. There may be only a few students interested in theories of general equilibrium, but many more care about government policy, the regulation of markets, minimum wages, health insurance, and used cars. Because more students are interested in the politics and the life of Thorstein Veblen than in the Arrow–Debreu theorem, we may better teach Arrow–Debreu by explaining first how Veblen's ideas of demand theory would violate what they say and their political goals.

Again and again, I teach aspects of microeconomics through controversy and use the history of thought to teach the underlying theory by discussing the evolution of the doctrine and challenges to it. I present the development of the discipline to uncover alternative approaches and to develop an alternative, institutional analysis. I do this for all three elements of the neoclassical system of price formation through supply and demand and market equilibrium.

3.1 Demand Theory

Even before I discuss the social construction of demand, I explore theories of preference formation in Léon Walras (or Paul Samuelson) and Thorstein Veblen. While some underlying preferences may be inherent in human genetics and biology, their manifestation is socially constructed. I discuss, for example, hair length and choice of clothes between men and women in the class. Even very low prices have little effect on many gender norms and consumer choices. Men, for example, *never* wear dresses to class, even if the price falls sharply and the weather gets very hot. Similarly, women very rarely cut their hair as short as men wear it; and, going on dates, they usually wear heels and make-up. Not only does society shape our behavior, it forms our opinions. I discuss behavioral experiments that have demonstrated that people not only *say* they enjoy wine more when they believe it is expensive, but brain scans indicate that they *feel* more pleasure from the same wine when they believe it is more expensive. I add to this lessons on the social origins of demand, discussing, for example, the spread of cell phones, and comparing beer and wine drinking on opposite sides of the Rhine to expose the role of state policy in promoting different forms of consumption in Bismarck's Germany and the French Third Republic.

While these findings are hard to explain assuming exogenous preferences, both Smith and Veblen agree that we consume for others as much as for ourselves. Our consumption is to impress upon others aspects of ourselves that we want them to accept. Social influences also affect demand in other ways because our consumption is a social act (Smith, 1892; Leibenstein, 1950). Of course, another aspect of Smith and Veblen demand theory is that we are often unaware of the value of goods and form expectations of fair prices from our neighbors' consumption. Beyond information, the pleasure we take from various activities depends on what our friends and others are doing. We are more likely to stay at a party, for example, when our friends are there; and less likely to go to class if we know they are skipping out. Similarly, we find various technologies more useful when our friends and neighbors use the same devices. Appliances using European-style cords or fixed wrenches set to metric measurements are more useful in France than in the United States. Many of my students use Microsoft products even while believing that others (Apple) are better because it is easier to collaborate and to work in networks where others use Microsoft. Consumption is a social act shaped by social institutions (the social influence is stressed by Durkheim, 1938, 1964).

Rather than jumping straight into the neoclassical supply and demand model, I go further with ideas from Smith and use the history of economic thought and the development of economics as a discipline to raise several other important issues in demand theory. Smith noted the advantage over barter of using money for market exchange, a point developed by Ronald Coase who elaborated on the idea of transactions costs standing between market buyers and sellers. Developing this concept, I discuss how social institutions, like common language, systems of weights and measures, and efficient police and judicial systems, affect a community's transactions costs. I also discuss how social norms and standards of honesty and trust influence the costs of using the market and protecting property. This last leads to another large policy issue, one raised by some recent scholars, like Sam Bowles, working in the transactions costs area: to what extent does using the market and relying on individual incentives undermine social norms of honesty and trust, thus undermining the efficiency of a market-based economy (Bowles, 2016)?

Social influences are also crucial for various products that cannot be treated as individual consumption. For example, drawing on writings from John Kenneth Galbraith and Coase to Robert Axelrod, I discuss public goods and externalities. I draw on a Socratic dialog to introduce the concept of the 'prisoner's dilemma' and show how this applies to a variety of social problems involving public goods and externalities. (Discussing his performance at the Battle of Delium in 424 BCE, Socrates notes that an individual soldier may anticipate doing better for himself by running from the fight, but if all do this, then the battle line will collapse and they will all be worse off.) I discuss Axelrod's work on the evolution of coop-eration to show how repeated contact, the establishment of lasting communities, contributes to resolving the prisoner's dilemma issues (Axelrod, 2006). I discuss the privatization of public goods, such as New York's Gramercy Park, and the meaning of the so-called Coase theorem. This is a good opportunity to teach opportunity costs and an interesting type of economic reasoning; it also allows us to relate the development of economic analysis to political debates and public policy on issues ranging from environmental policy to town–gown controversies over student drinking and late-night partying.

Social influences on demand and public policy are also central to the work of feminist economists from Charlotte Perkins Gilman through Nancy Folbre (Gilman, 1975; Folbre, 2012). We discuss the 'care economy' and the provision of care labor through the market and through families and other social bodies. While this builds on the discussion of public goods and transactions costs, it introduces several other important ideas, including idiosyncratic exchange, where a participant to an exchange depends on the exchange being with a particular party, thus establishing a degree of monopoly power and reducing the possibility for what Albert Hirschman called market 'exit' and requiring the exercise of 'voice' (Hirschman, 2004). In addition, there are problems with using markets in the care economy because of problems with the initial distribution, initial endowments, and problems with credit markets. Children are par-ticularly dependent and need care but also lack resources, or access to credit markets to borrow against future income, to pay their care givers. This leads to problems of third-party payment, or dependence on charity, either from parents and other family members or 'the kindness of strangers.'

This excursion into the history of thought suggests limits to a supply and demand framework and problems if a society relies on individual incentives to supply important goods and services. Having inoculated students against being seduced by the simple elegance of the neoclassical system, I then present neoclassical demand. I start with marginal utility as in Jevons, John Bates Clark, or Paul Samuelson in order to develop downward-sloping demand curves. The point is not merely to contrast upward- and downward-sloping individual demand or social demand, but to demonstrate that supply and demand is an important concept to understand, precisely *because* it is controversial. I draw on Clark's own lecture notes to discuss why Robinson Crusoe would value additional coconuts at an ever diminishing rate, and how he would work less hard to get more. We thus build the downward sloping demand curve on the basis of diminishing marginal utility for an isolated individual. I discuss with students the extent to which this can be generalized to a community of connected individuals, or to other types of products. Under circumstances with imperfect information, network economies, or Veblen effects, the community demand curve may not be a simple sum of individual demands.

3.2 Theory of Supply

I present market supply through a prism of the history of thought and the evolution of ideas about individualist and social determinants of production. Again, I begin with Adam Smith and his theory of the productivity gains from the division of labor. I begin with a downward-sloping production possibility frontier (PPF), guns and butter, as dominated the thinking of Soviet planners in the five-year plans or American war production planners in the 1940s. I contrast this with Smith's idea that 'the division of labor is limited by the extent of the market' and, therefore, greater demand can elicit greater supply. For Smith, productivity comes from greater exchange, and division of labor, and increased production of one good can lead to greater production of the other. Different goods can be complements rather than substitutes and, therefore, may have an upward-sloping PPF.[1]

Thinking of classical versus neoclassical theory, I carefully distinguish between the economic 'short run,' popular with neoclassical thinkers, where many inputs are fixed, and the classical theorists' 'long run,' where all vary. As in the discussion of demand, the point is to establish the conditions for a market equilibrium, and to evaluate the value in policy making of using a supply and demand framework. I begin with Karl Marx and John Bates Clark and the dispute over labor exploitation. While Marx, building on Smith, attributed all value to labor, and therefore concluded that all profit came from exploitation, Clark developed an alternative theory where profit came from the productive contribution of capital and was therefore innocent of any abusive aspect. There is a metaphysics here, and a full discussion of the implications and of the 'Cambridge capital controversies' is far beyond any intro course, but the point for my class is that Clark's work, like Marx's, is fundamentally political.

Deriving the product supply curve from the production function involves some algebra but is a useful exercise because it shows the limits of Clark's approach. Clark goes, of course, from diminishing marginal productivity of variable factors to rising marginal costs and upward-sloping short-run supply curves. Reconstructing his marginal cost curve demonstrates how the theory is for the short run because, in the long run, marginal products are not downward sloping because there need not be any change in the ratio of factor inputs. This leads to a point made by John Maurice Clark, son of John Bates: long-run marginal cost curves are not upward sloping and, therefore, in the long run, supply curves are flat or downward sloping. And we thus return to the classical system where prices are set by the costs of production.

This approach lays the groundwork for introducing the idea of endogenous supply and long-term economic growth. Here, again, I draw on Adam Smith who laid out the conditions for long-term growth where he says that '[t]he greatest improvement in the productive powers of labour ... have been the effects of the division of labour' and the division of labor is limited 'by the extent of the market' (Smith, 1776, pp. 8, 18). In addition to emphasizing the role of wider trade and the importance of low-cost transportation, this is an argument for self-sustaining or *endogenous* growth because a larger volume of output allows for greater mechanization and extended division of labor leading to increased productivity through learning by doing. This is, of course, an idea that should be easily understood by college students. Not only does practice make violinists ready for Carnegie Hall, it makes workers better at their tasks and facilitates the discovery and implementation of the abundance of little technological innovations that promote long-term growth. 'Learning,' Kenneth Arrow argued half a century ago, 'is the product of experience. Learning can only take place through the attempt to solve a problem and therefore only takes place during activity'

(Arrow, 1962, p. 155). Learning to be more productive only happens when people are working; and when they are working, learning happens. After discussing Arrow's concept of learning by doing, I discuss case studies, such as the building of Liberty ships in World War II and technological progress in the semi-conductor industry. From Smith and Arrow, we have a new Say's Law: demand creates its own supply.

I draw on this debate among economists over the sources of growth because it highlights a divide between those who emphasize factor endowments, the provision of capital inputs, and technological progress, and among those who believe in technological progress between those who emphasize exogenous invention and learning by doing. By separating production from social conditions, the factor endowments case or the study of exogenous invention moves us back to the theoretical realm of Robinson Crusoe; learning, by contrast, puts us in the world of living people and shared experience.

4   MARKET EQUILIBRIUM IS SOCIAL, AND SO IS THE DISTRIBUTION OF INCOME

Having derived the conditions for the orthodox system of demand and supply, conditions founded on methodological individualism, I discuss market equilibrium, beginning with the early twentieth-century debate over market equilibrium. The neoclassical system assumes a large number of small competing firms. I compare this with the modern corporation, drawing on the writings of Richard Ely, John Maurice Clark, Joseph Schumpeter, and Adolph Berle and Gardiner Means. From this institutionalist tradition in American economics I discuss theories of imperfect competition, including those of the New Deal economists around Franklin Roosevelt. Rather than beginning with the admittedly unrealistic system of perfect competition, I start with the general case of imperfect competition where perfect competition is a special case with a large number of anonymous producers of homogeneous products. We derive marginal revenue curves and demonstrate how the market equilibrium differs between imperfect competition, with a downward-sloping marginal revenue (MR) curve, and perfect competition, where the MR curve is flat. We discuss the comparative equilibrium for monopoly and for perfect competition and compare social surplus.

This leads to the conclusion that markets may not maximize social surplus; and that regulation may lead to a socially better outcome.

Having grounded an alternative equilibrium based on a social model of demand and supply against an individualist neoclassical model, I discuss theories of price formation and income distribution. In the orthodox system, income is distributed according to relative productivity, individual preferences, and consumer sovereignty. In the institutionalist approach, however, distribution is a result of social choice and political decisions. I use Arthur Okun, especially *Equality and Efficiency*, as a frame for discussing inequality and the distribution of income (Okun, 1975). The conditions where income distribution will be set according to marginal productivity in perfectly competitive markets are particularly restrictive, and even in those a case can be made for redistributive policies. (I discuss theories from Rawls, 1971 and Nozick, 2013.) Alternatively, of course, if distribution is *not* set by fair market competition, then the case for redistribution is even stronger.

4.1 More on Labor Markets

Students want good jobs and high wages at 'high-road' companies. This makes the discussion of labor markets especially relevant to them. Having already discussed the orthodox marginal productivity theory, I show how this becomes a theory of labor demand. Before letting students accept marginal productivity as a theory of wage determination, however, I discuss caveats coming from the determinants of labor supply and from theories of efficiency wages.

Labor market outcomes depend on supply as well as demand, and supply is shaped by social policy determining the supply of competing and complementary labor to particular occupations. Students have observed and even experienced discrimination, on the basis of ethnicity, gender, race, sexual orientation, among others. I introduce labor market discrimination in terms of income differentials for different groups, America's history of racial and religious discrimination, the theories of Gary Becker, and the experience of Jackie Robinson and the Brooklyn Dodgers (Becker, 1957). Beyond any 'taste for discrimination,' I discuss the steering of people into different occupational tracks and the effects of crowding on wages for women and other groups. From there it is a short step to discussing winners and losers from discrimination, ranging from the owners of

Negro League teams to consumers of the care services provided by women as well as mediocre white baseball players and men who are able to get good jobs as plumbers and surgeons only because otherwise qualified women are steered elsewhere.

Labor supply also depends on the population and the legal environment around immigration. I begin by discussing the currently popular idea that immigration lowers wages, and show how this relies on particularly simple supply and demand analysis. Then I discuss how results change when we consider different types of workers with different degrees of substitutability and complementarity in the work. From this we arrive at a much more complicated, and realistic view of immigration: native-born workers benefit or lose from immigration depending on the degree to which the work done by immigrants is complementary or a substitute for their own work (compare Borjas and Katz, 2007; and Ottaviano and Peri, 2012).

Finally, I use the work of Larry Summers, and others, to reverse Clark's causality and argue that higher wages *cause* higher productivity. Like others before me, I start with Henry Ford and his $5/day to show how higher wages can cause productivity-raising better morale (Raff and Summers, 1987; Wolfers and Zilinsky, 2015). We can then discuss good jobs, bad jobs, and high-road and low-road employers, and where the students themselves want to work. To explain wage and income disparities, these are vital issues. For our students, it may suffice to note that economics does not get much more relevant than this.

5 STUDENTS CAN APPRECIATE A BETTER ECONOMICS, AN ECONOMICS MEANINGFUL IN THEIR OWN EXPERIENCE

Teaching a better economics, one that recognizes controversy and the role of experience and institutions in market outcomes, requires that students learn more, but we should not be deterred by the risk that we will be making our courses more difficult for students. In narrow, ahistorical orthodox economics classes, much time is spent explaining to students that they should ignore things that they *know* are important because they are left out of our abstract model. This extreme abstraction contributes to student frustration with our models. The failure of our models to explain the world or provide a useful guide to policy making has contributed to growing frustration with our teaching. Leading economists have long complained of the narrowness of our teaching (see, for example, the signers of the petition in Hodgson, Mäki and McCloskey, 1992). Especially since the current economic crisis began, they have been joined by growing numbers of students who are demanding a more realistic and more relevant economics (Pilling, 2016; International Student Initiative for Pluralism in Economics, 2016; Rethinking Economics, 2016; Ruccio, 2016).[2] These students are not looking for an *easier* economics; they are looking for a better economics.

There is an obvious challenge in making our models more realistic: there are entire areas of 'facts' that we need to consider and our models are no longer simple but can reach different conclusions depending on circumstances and experience. But, for the students, there is much to be gained from our teaching an economics that is more meaningful to them. Instead of relying on an abstract analysis that contradicts their own experience, a historical and institutional analysis can be easier for them to grasp.

Colleagues, including those teaching intermediate microeconomics, may question whether it is appropriate to spend so much time on matters of historical doctrine and material outside the mainstream. They would ask whether there is enough time in an introductory course to cover the orthodox model *and* everything else that I am adding in. To these questions I could respond snidely that students learn very little in conventional introductory economics courses so there is little to lose. More to the point, by adding context and controversy, we make the course more engaging and more meaningful. Students are more likely to learn the orthodox model when they see a reason for it; they are more likely to learn the orthodox model when they are exposed to its challenges.

NOTES

1. I will also mention certain products, like apples and honey, which are production complements.
2. A group of economists has even launched a comedy troupe to mock the prevailing mainstream (Kilkenomics Festival: The World's First Economics and Comedy Festival, 2016).

REFERENCES

Arrow, K.J. (1962), 'The economic implications of learning by doing', *The Review of Economic Studies*, **29**(3), 155–73.

Axelrod, R.M. (2006), *The Evolution of Cooperation*, New York: Basic Books.

Becker, G.S. (1957), *The Economics of Discrimination*, Chicago, IL: University of Chicago Press.

Borjas, G. and L. Katz (2007), *Mexican Immigration to the United States*, Chicago, IL: University of Chicago Press.

Bowles, S. (2016), *The Moral Economy: Why Good Incentives Are No Substitute for Good Citizens*, New Haven, CT: Yale University Press.

Durkheim, E. (1938), *The Rules of Sociological Method*, 8th edition, Chicago, IL: University of Chicago Press.

Durkheim, E. (1964), *The Division of Labor in Society*, New York: Free Press of Glencoe.

Folbre, N. (2012), *For Love and Money: Care Provision in the United States*, New York: Russell Sage Foundation.

Friedman, G. (2015), *Microeconomics: Individual Choice in Communities*, 2nd edition, Boston, MA: Dollars & Sense.

Gilman, C.P. (1975), *Women and Economics: A Study of the Economic Relation Between Men and Women as a Factor in Social Evolution*, 9th edition, New York: Gordon Press.

Hirschman, A.O. (1977), *The Passions and the Interests: Political Arguments for Capitalism Before Its Triumph*, Princeton, NJ: Princeton University Press.

Hirschman, A.O. (2004), *Exit, Voice, and Loyalty: Responses to Decline in Firms, Organizations, and States*, Cambridge, MA: Harvard University Press.

Hodgson, G., U. Mäki and D. McCloskey (1992), 'A plea for a pluralistic and rigorous economics', *American Economic Review*, **88**(2), xxv, accessed December 16, 2017 at https://www.scribd.com/document/332086319/Plea-for-a-pluralistic-and-rigorous-economics.

International Student Initiative for Pluralism in Economics (2016), 'Member groups', accessed December 8, 2017 at http://www.isipe.net/member-groups/.

Kilkenomics Festival: The World's First Economics and Comedy Festival (2016), brochure, accessed December 8, 2017 at https://www.kilkenomics.com/wp-content/uploads/2016/11/Kilkenomics-Brochure-2016.pdf.

Leibenstein, H. (1950), 'Bandwagon, snob, and Veblen effects in the theory of consumers' demand', *The Quarterly Journal of Economics*, **64**(2), 183–207.

Mill, J.S. (1978), *On Liberty*, Indianapolis: Hackett Publishing Company.

Nozick, R. (2013), *Anarchy, State, and Utopia*, New York: Basic Books.

Okun, A.M. (1975), *Equality and Efficiency: The Big Tradeoff*, Washington, DC: Brookings Institution.

Ottaviano, G.I.P. and G. Peri (2012), 'Rethinking the effect of immigration on wages', *Journal of the European Economic Association*, **10**(1), 152–97.

Pilling, D. (2016), 'Crash and learn: Should we change the way we teach economics?', *Financial Times*, September 30, accessed October 23, 2016 at https://www.ft.com/content/0dc9b416-8573-11e6-8897-2359a58ac7a5.

Raff, D.M.G. and L.H. Summers (1987), 'Did Henry Ford pay efficiency wages?', *Journal of Labor Economics*, **5**(4), 57–86.

Rawls, J. (1971), *A Theory of Justice*, Cambridge, MA: Belknap Press of Harvard University Press.

Rethinking Economics (2016), website, accessed December 8, 2017 at http://www.rethinkeconomics.org/.

Ruccio, D. (2016), 'Crash and learn?', *Real-World Economics Review Blog*, October 7, accessed December 16, 2017 at https://rwer.wordpress.com/2016/10/07/crash-and-learn/.

Smith, A. (1776), *An Inquiry into the Nature and Causes of the Wealth of Nations*, accessed December 16, 2017 at http://www.econlib.org/library/Smith/smWN.html.

Smith, A. (1892), *The Theory of Moral Sentiments; to Which Is Added, a Dissertation on the Origin of Languages*, new edition (Bohn's Standard Library), London: G. Bell & Sons.

Wolfers, J. and J. Zilinsky (2015), 'Higher wages for low-income workers lead to higher productivity', *PIIE*, January 13, accessed December 16, 2017 at https://piie.com/blogs/realtime-economic-issues-watch/higher-wages-low-income-workers-lead-higher-productivity.

7. Teaching money and banking with regard to the history of economic thought

Louis-Philippe Rochon and Sergio Rossi

1 INTRODUCTION

Most textbooks today still present the quantity of money as an exogenous variable under the control of central banks. Yet, historians have found no evidence supporting this claim, which then prompts the question: where did this idea originate?

True, the exogeneity of money is a logical necessity of neoclassical theory: as inflation is seen as the result of an excess supply of money, neoclassical economists must give themselves the means by which money can be controlled, otherwise their argument is a non sequitur. And while central banks are themselves recognizing the endogenous nature of money, at least in a Wicksellian sense, textbooks are slow to recognize this fact and still portray the money supply as a vertical curve in interest rate/money space. As a result, students get their degrees in economics with the illusion that central banks are in command of the growth of the money supply.

Post-Keynesian and other heterodox approaches, however, consider money rather as an endogenous variable. To support this view, this chapter focuses on the importance of teaching money and banking with regard to the history of economic thought, to show that the nature of money and the role of banks have been essentially misunderstood to date in the economics profession. This erroneous understanding of money, in turn, gave rise to a variety of monetary policy interventions, both in the distant past and more recently, that were not (and could not be) up to the task. The chapter explains thus why a sound understanding of the properties of money and banking is crucial for economic analysis as well as policy making.

The next section presents the mainstream view with respect to money and banking, as it is taught in orthodox courses at academic level. It argues that neither the commodity money approach nor the view that considers money as an asset is in a position to grasp the essential nature of money as a book entry. As a result, the conventional argument that banks are merely financial intermediaries, similar to other (non-bank) financial institutions, is wrong. Hence, policies based on this approach are doomed to fail, and may in fact exacerbate the economic situation. This explains why a number of past and present banking regulations are not appropriate in order to avoid a (systemic) financial crisis to occur, contrary to the well-established belief in Basel III-like agreements and ensuing microprudential (or even macroprudential) policy tools, which are studied at academic level as if they were the appropriate (market-based) solution to avoid further systemic crises. The third section presents the classical theory of money, to point out that it deserves to be considered anew by teachers in relation to a number of issues in the mainstream view of money and banking. For instance, Smith's ([1776] 1991, pp. 254–5) appraisal of money as 'the great wheel of circulation', as well as his conceptual distinction between 'money' and 'money's worth' (ibid.), are two examples that show to teachers and their students the relevance of a theoretical approach that considers money and production as the two fundamental elements of any economic systems in the actual world. In this perspective, the third section also discusses the controversies between the Banking and Currency Schools, aiming at explaining thereby the particular nature of banks in a monetary economy of production. The fourth section elaborates on this, presenting the most advanced heterodox theories of money, which have been proposed by post-Keynesians and monetary circuit theorists. It points out that money does not exist because of agents' liquidity preference, but because it is a means of final payment that any kinds of agents, including banks, need to settle their own debt obligations. The fourth section notably argues that (bank) money is endogenous not as a result of an evolutionary process as claimed by Chick (1986), but because of its essential role in any payments system. The conclusion, which builds on Rochon and Rossi (2013), points out that it is fundamental that money and banking are understood by teachers and researchers, as well as policy makers in any economic domains.

2 THE MAINSTREAM VIEW OF MONEY AND BANKING

Teaching money and banking to economics students is both exciting and amazing, since it helps them discover and understand the essential nature of money as well as the specific functions of banks. A suitable teaching strategy in this connection is to refer to the history of monetary thinking, to point out that money has been a core issue across the whole spectrum of economic theories, even before banks as such appeared on Earth. This teaching strategy is also instrumental in showing how important it is, for students, to develop their conceptual rigour and logical thinking, in order to understand and analyse money and banking correctly. An appropriate starting point for this teaching strategy to be successful is to present the orthodox approach to money and banking critically. This introduces students to neoclassical money-using economic models, without the need to bother them with algebra and econometrics – both of which cannot help people understand what money actually is.

The current mainstream view of money and banking can be traced back to monetarism, which is itself a revised version of the quantity theory of money (see Rossi, forthcoming) that was proposed in the eighteenth century by Hume ([1752] 1955) when money was reified as precious metals like gold and silver: in this sense, many claimed that money had intrinsic value. At that time, it was therefore normal to believe that the supply of money might have depended on the availability of the material that was used to carry out money's functions – which indeed has been considered by several authors, like Hicks (1967, p. 1), as instrumental in defining money's nature. This approach is still in fashion, as the large majority of economists today define money simply according to its functions: as the old expression claims, 'money is what money does' (Walker, 1880, p. 1). Teachers of economics, however, should be aware that this definition of money is prone to circularity and, hence, is analytically useless. Indeed, as Bofinger (2001, p. 4) has argued, '[i]f it is not clear what "money" is, it is also not possible to describe the functions of "money"'. Once students have been exposed to this logical critique to the mainstream view of money, they can understand why it is wrong to maintain (as many orthodox economists do) that money's value depends on its scarcity with respect to other (non-monetary) items – like goods, services or assets – which orthodox authors consider are merely exchanged against money in a bilateral transaction involving two agents. This amounts to the view that money enters any exchange as the general equivalent of goods and services, which orthodox economists usually assume to be given in the 'initial endowments' of agents – who thereby maximize their own utility through entering into exchange in the marketplace.

In this perspective, as Fisher ([1911] 1931, p. 2, original emphasis) maintained, 'any commodity to be called "money" must be *generally acceptable in exchange*, and any commodity generally acceptable in exchange should be called money'. The commodity money view stems from what Servet (1994, p. 103, our translation) has called 'the myth of barter': money would have emerged from a barter trade system, once agents became aware that the so-called 'double coincidence of wants' (Jevons, 1875, p. 3) represented a severe constraint on their utility maximization. To reduce this market friction, agents were thus led to accept some particular commodities, like grain, metals or empty shells, in exchange for those goods and services they offered, provided that these commodities were generally accepted in exchange. According to Hayek (1933, p. 44), this gave rise to 'indirect exchange', as money 'enables the act of purchase to be separated from the act of sale' (Friedman, 1974, p. 8). As a result, '[m]oney is treated as a stock, not as a flow or a mixture of a flow and a stock' (Friedman, 1987, p. 5).

In addressing the shortcomings of Friedman's view, economic history can help both teachers and their students, considering the gradual dematerialization that occurred over time of money's physical supports. Indeed, the historical evolution of money's physical representations has led several mainstream economists to adjust their views of money. They have thus followed the alleged empirical evidence that money is an asset based on trust (that is, on a social convention), since its purchasing power does not depend any more on the material that carries out money's functions. Framed by general equilibrium theory, which views money as a physical numéraire, the mainstream view of money as an asset boils down to considering that any exchange where money intervenes, hence a payment, involves two agents and two separate objects of exchange. As Hicks (1967, p. 3) pointed out in this regard, 'although Walras does take one of his *n* commodities as numéraire (or unit of account) it is an essential part of his theory that the numéraire does not enter into the exchange in any different way from any other of the commodities'. As a matter of fact, it is easy to point out to students that, in neoclassical economics, '[t]he numéraire is not money; it is not even a partial money; it is not even assumed that it is used by the traders themselves as a unit of account. It is not more than a unit of account which the observing economist is using for his own purpose of explaining to himself what the traders are doing' (ibid.). Within general equilibrium analysis, students are thus in a position to understand that money is inessential in the sense of Hahn (1973, p. 231): the role of money as an asset is not instrumental in determining the models' solution (Rogers, 1989, p. 63). This asset is simply considered as the general equivalent of non-monetary goods that are exchanged against it. In such a framework, as famously pointed out by Hicks (1967, p. 3), teachers can easily explain to their students that '[a]ny of the other $n-1$ commodities might have been taken as numéraire'. Hence, students are led to notice that mainstream monetary models are essentially barter models, since '"money" may always be added [to them] without altering any of the perfect barter results' (Rogers, 1989, p. 46).

At this stage, students can fully understand that orthodox economists consider banks as simply a category of financial intermediaries among others, because they imagine that banks need to collect available savings in order to open credit lines to any potential (creditworthy) borrowers. Money-and-banking teachers can thus explain the origins of the loanable-funds theory, according to which saving is really instrumental in order for investment to occur, as in the IS–LM model that many economics teachers still use to introduce their students to macroeconomic analysis (see Cencini, 2003 for a radical critique of this model). In this framework, students learn that the rate of interest is an endogenous variable, resulting from the supply of savings and the demand for loanable funds. They are told that a central bank, in such a framework, cannot but fix the policy rate of interest at the level of the market rate of interest – also called the 'natural' rate of interest by mainstream economists such as Woodford (2003), because it makes sure that saving and investment are at equilibrium (see Massonnet, 2015, for critical elaboration on this) – in order not to disturb the path to full employment equilibrium that the market mechanism provides over the long run, according to the mainstream view. In this regard teachers should point out that this perspective reproduces the quantity theory of money view that assumes money to be neutral as regards so-called real magnitudes, like output and employment levels – whose equilibrium value is determined by the mechanism of supply and demand in the marketplace.

In this perspective, where banks are simply financial intermediaries between savers and investors, their activities must not be regulated by imposing any stringent liquidity ratio or minimum capital requirement (such as those introduced by Basel agreements I to III; see Cardim de Carvalho, 2015), because these regulations hinder channelling savings to finance investment and are therefore considered as a drag on economic growth. In fact, this perspective is flawed on logical and conceptual grounds, as the next section points out, referring to the classical analysis of money and banking.

3   THE CLASSICAL ANALYSIS OF MONEY AND BANKING

The classical analysis of money and banking provides several clues to understanding the true nature of both of them, and to reject thereby the mainstream paradigm that informs the current political debate and economic policy stance around the world. It is therefore worthwhile for teachers as well as scholars to consider the classical monetary literature, as it provides a better starting point from which to understand the essential nature of money and the role of banks.

An appropriate starting point in teaching the classical analysis of money is Adam Smith, who was already aware of the vehicular essence of money. In his own words, 'money, by means of which the whole revenue of the society is regularly distributed among all its different members, makes itself no part of that revenue. The great wheel of circulation is altogether different from the goods which are circulated by means of it' (Smith [1776] 1991, p. 254). In this quote, Smith argues that money has no value at all, since it is merely the vehicle of those goods and services that it circulates. Recall that in mainstream theory, money is used in exchange for goods and services, such that money and goods move in opposite directions. Yet, for Smith, this is not the case and students then easily understand it is not logically possible to maintain – as mainstream economists have been doing all the time – that money is a stock magnitude entering into exchange as the general equivalent of those non-monetary items exchanged against it in the marketplace. To make this point more convincingly, teachers can refer to the fact that a vehicle (money) carries its own load (goods and services), both of which move logically in the same direction and not one against the other. This thereby leads students to also reject the orthodox idea that monetary flows depict the circulation of the stock of money, that is to say, money 'on the wing', as Robertson (1937, p. 29) famously called it. Essentially, in fact, money is not a stock magnitude, but a flow that carries to agents something, that is to say, goods, services and (real or financial) assets. Money is worthless (devoid of intrinsic value) because its purchasing power stems from the objects that it carries as a purely numerical vehicle (and which define its extrinsic value). This is a logical conclusion to which students in money and banking should be led by their teachers, referring to the classical writings in the history of monetary thought.

Indeed, Smith ([1776] 1991, p. 255) made it clear that money must be distinguished from money's worth conceptually: 'the wealth or revenue ... is equal only to one of the two values which are thus intimated somewhat ambiguously by the same word, and to the latter more properly than to the former, to the money's worth more properly than to the money'. Smith was thus aware that the purchasing power of money stems neither from the material that carries out money's functions nor from a social convention, but rather from the link between money and production established by the payment of wages that occurs on the labour market: 'though the wages of the workman are commonly paid to him in money, his real revenue, like that of all other men, consists, not in the money, but in the money's worth; not in the metal pieces, but in what can be got for them' (p. 260). This is a fundamental idea that has been adopted by proponents of the so-called monetary circuit (see Rochon, 1999; Graziani, 2003).

This analysis allows teachers to explain the debates between the Currency School and the Banking School that occurred during the nineteenth century (see Figuera, 2015). For proponents of the former, which adhered to the quantity theory of money, central banks (namely, the Bank of England at that time) must avoid money overissuance by linking money emission to a strict rule such as the gold standard, in order to make sure that price stability prevails (as argued by Ricardo [1810–11] 2004, and Torrens, 1837, among others). In this view, as Friedman (1987, p. 17, original emphasis) famously claimed, '*inflation is always and everywhere a monetary phenomenon* in the sense that it is and can be produced only by a more rapid increase in the quantity of money than in output'. Central banks must thus abide by a rule – like the so-called 'Friedman rule'

– that can guarantee price stability by increasing the money supply in line with actual output growth (see Mihailov, 2015).

Proponents of the Banking School, by contrast, rejected this approach, arguing that the emission of money is an endogenous phenomenon that banks carry out with respect to the 'needs of trade', independently of the monetary regime and the policy stance of the central bank (see, for instance, Tooke, 1844, and Fullarton, 1845). In this view, teachers can explain that banks are special, because – contrary to non-bank financial institutions – they can issue money via the credit lines they decide to grant to any kind of economic agents, without having the constraint to finance these lines of credit with pre-existent savings. Now, rather than trying to validate one school of thought or the other by referring to monetary history (see Knodell, 2017), which can never be considered as sufficient to establish their validity on scientific grounds, teachers of money and banking could refer to logical thinking in order to assess whether bank loans make bank deposits (as argued by the Banking School) or the other way round (as imagined by the Currency School). This is the approach adopted by many heterodox schools of thought, to which we now turn in order to provide a sound explanation of money and banking, which economics teachers can easily use to discard the mainstream view of both of them.

4   MONEY AND BANKING IN HETERODOX ECONOMICS

Referring to heterodox economics in order to teach money and banking allows one to explain that they are two closely related objects of analysis. This is because heterodox economics considers production and financial market activities as crucial to explain the working of real-world economic systems; that is, a variety of issues such as inflation, unemployment, financial bubbles and crises (see Cencini and Rossi, 2015). Indeed, both production and financial transactions need banks and money in order to function. This puts money and banking at centre stage in both theory and policy making (Rochon, 1999). Rather than introducing money later in the analysis, as does neoclassical economics by treating money as a simple after-thought,[1] economics teachers must explain to students that money in fact must be introduced at the very beginning of the discussion, or 'on the very ground floor of our analytic structure', as Schumpeter (1954, p. 278) urges us to do. Hence money and banking must feature in each introductory economics course – and should be explained by thoroughly adopting a pluralistic approach that refers to the history of economic thought (see Rossi, 2012).[2]

First of all, heterodox economics helps teachers to emphasize that it is necessary to have a logically correct conception of money in order to understand its nature, issuance, and purchasing power. Contrary to the mainstream paradigm, which assumes the purchasing power of money but cannot explain it logically as recalled above, heterodox economics, and particularly monetary circuit theory (see Rochon, 1999; Parguez and Seccareccia, 2000; Graziani, 2003) and quantum macroeconomics (see Cencini, 2005; Rossi, 2007; Bailly, Cencini and Rossi, 2017), explain that money's purchasing power stems from production – that is, from the payment of wages on the labour market. Students understand immediately that it is indeed the workers' intellectual as well as physical effort that originates output – that is, an economic object that is valuable as it associates a numerical form (money) to its real content (produced goods or services). As a matter of fact, this association exists in the form of bank deposits, which are indeed the financial representation of produced output – hence a claim to it in the hands of deposit holders. This is why it is important for teachers to distinguish money (a purely numerical form, or a flow) from bank deposits (a stock of purchasing power), in order to avoid considering, in full contrast with reality, that banks may originate a purchasing power by a stroke of the pen (or keyboard). To be sure, banks issue the means of payment, but the object of this payment is a good, service or asset that cannot but stem from production originally. This allows teachers to explain why it is necessary to start from the analysis of production to understand the nature of money and its purchasing power. Students will thereby understand that the monetary theory of production that Keynes ([1933] 1973) put to the fore, and monetary circuit theorists à la Graziani (1990) elaborated upon, is an appropriate starting point from which to understand money and banking in any capitalist systems. In fact, it is the starting point of understanding capitalism itself.

In this regard, teachers can point out that (following the approach adopted by classical economists) monetary circuit theorists and heterodox economists in general consider the economic system as a whole and focus on the macroeconomic relationships between its different categories of agents, to wit, workers, firms, and the banking sector, or what Graziani (1990, p. 8) has called 'macro-groups'. Students can easily understand that these categories of agents enter into several transactions across a variety of markets such as the labour market, the product market, and the financial market. For the sake of simplicity, teachers may ignore the public sector and the foreign sector – even though it would be possible to integrate both of them in the monetary circuit framework without losing consistency (see, for example, Di Lorenzo, 2014).

In such a framework, the first analytical step teachers must address is to investigate the labour market, where the newly produced output appears (as an economic object) as soon as wages are paid out by firms to workers through the banking sector as a whole. In this regard, teachers will have to explain that banks provide both money and credit to firms, in order for the latter to compensate wage earners for their efforts in producing any kinds of goods or services, which firms sell to households on the product market, thereby allowing them to reimburse banks' credit lines. Students thus notice that the monetary circuit is actually a circuit of income, because the latter is created on the labour market when the payment of wages occurs, and destroyed on the product market when households buy the output sold by firms. As Keynes (1936, pp. 213–14) argued, labour is the only true factor of production because it alone is able to create value within the economic system. Teachers should point out, however, that this process of value creation does not refer to physical magnitudes, because output is the result of just a transformation of matter and energy: it concerns the creation of national income, which is the economic result of money and production being associated through the payment of wages on the labour market. Students will thereby easily understand that this is actually a macroeconomic process, as it involves the economic system as a whole and gives rise to an income that is new, and net, for the whole economy (Cencini and Rossi, 2015, pp. 22–30). This is recorded by banks in the form of new deposits within their ledgers, thereby confirming that loans make deposits in banks' books and not the other way round (see above). The first stage of the monetary circuit is thus over when wage earners receive a claim on a bank deposit as a result of the firms' compensation of their efforts. This is a purchasing power that exists in the form of bank deposits, which are therefore a stock magnitude – to be distinguished from money, which is a flow that vehiculates to the payees (to wit, wage earners) their claim on produced output stocked in the firms' inventories waiting to be sold on the market for produced goods and services. Some post-Keynesians, such as Lavoie (1999, 2014) and Rochon (1999), have argued that money is both a flow and a stock, an argument that students can better understand once they distinguish money from bank deposits as explained above.

The above discussion makes clear the flow nature of money, and makes it evident that economic agents do not demand money as a result of their liquidity preferences (as claimed, for instance, by Chick and Dow, 2002), but rather because they need money as a means of final payment first and foremost. The latter occurs indeed when 'a seller of a good, or service, or another asset, receives something of equal value from the purchaser, which leaves the seller with no further claim on the buyer' (Goodhart, 1989, p. 26). This explains that banks neither buy nor sell anything when they issue money in order for a payment to occur finally. Banks just provide the numerical counter needed to measure, in economic terms, the object(s) of the relevant transaction between the buyer and the seller. This also makes it plain that each payment involves three parties rather than two: the payer, the payee, and the banking sector as a go-between (Hicks, 1967, p. 11). As Parguez and Seccareccia (2000, p. 101) have also argued, '"money" is a by-product of a balance-sheet operation of a third agent who, in modern parlance, can be dubbed a "bank"'.

As a matter of fact, banks are both money and credit providers ('The Part Played by the Banking System', Keynes, 1973, p. 91): money as well as credit are determined endogenously, so that banks are both monetary and financial intermediaries. As monetary intermediaries, banks issue money starting from scratch, providing loans that give rise to bank deposits as a result of production. As financial intermediaries, by way of contrast, banks collect savings to refinance ex post their lending with produced income. In the former case, banks record income as the result of any production activities. In the latter case, banks vehiculate pre-existent savings to any borrower that is deemed creditworthy by banks' managers – and even to non-creditworthy borrowers as a result of securitization, which moved banks from the originate-and-hold model to the more profitable (but much riskier) originate-and-distribute model (see Rossi, 2011, for analytical elaboration).

The nature of money as a purely numerical flow that banks issue whenever they record the result of a payment, makes it easy for students to understand that money is indeed an endogenous magnitude, because it is the result of a demand for it every time a payment needs to be carried out. Students will thereby understand that money's endogeneity does not depend on the historical period, as claimed, for instance, by Chick (1986), but stems from money's nature – which has not been altered over time, even though the material form used to represent money has evolved in economic history (see Rochon and Rossi, 2013). Hence, rather than considering the evolutionary theory of money as suggested by Chick (1986), who simply focuses on surface phenomena such as the material form of money and the institution in charge of it, teachers should explain endogenous money as an essential feature of every monetary economy, both in ancient history and in modern times – what Rochon and Rossi (2013) have called the 'revolutionary' theory of endogenous money. As Lavoie (1996, p. 533) points out, referring to the intense debates between so-called structuralists and horizontalists in post-Keynesian monetary economics (see Rochon and Rossi, 2017), 'accommodation or the lack of it, liability management or the lack of it, and financial innovations or the lack of it are second-order phenomena compared to the crucial story that goes from debt creation to the supply of means of payment'. This clearly means that the emission of money is an entirely endogenous phenomenon, irrespective of central bank behaviour, the stage of development of the banking sector, financial innovations, and more recent micro- and macroprudential regulations (Rochon and Rossi, 2013).

5   CONCLUSION

The analysis presented in this chapter has shown that money and banking are essential – both for the working of any economic systems and for understanding how these systems actually work. Teachers of economics should resist the temptation to explain money and banking using a mathematical approach that cannot capture the essence of both of them. A much more useful approach to understanding the nature of money and the role of banks is thus to consider the history of economic thought, because there are several strands of thought that can help explain this subject matter on logical grounds. Logic and conceptual rigour, rather than mathematics and econometric techniques, are indeed the keys to understanding that money is a purely numerical entry in banks' books, whose purchasing power cannot stem from either a social convention or the material that carries out money's function as a means of payment. A bookkeeping approach to money, nevertheless, is not enough, as banks' ledgers record the result of money's emission – that is, a stock magnitude in the form of bank deposits – rather than the emission of money as such, which is a flow that cannot be captured by the traditional double-entry bookkeeping. This is why a logical reasoning is required, to see that banks create the number of money units that measure the value of the objects of the relevant transaction, but can never create the purchasing power that is necessary in order for this transaction to be finally paid. Conceptual rigour enables one to distinguish the means of final payment (money) from the result of such a payment (bank deposits). It can be further enhanced by a critical appraisal of the history of economic thought, provided it considers that surface phenomena – like the exchange between money and non-monetary items (such as goods, services and assets) – are of no help to grasp the underlying nature of the payment that this exchange simply reveals. A logically sound and rigorous conceptual framework must be provided first. Indeed, this is instrumental in grasping the particular nature of money independently of its (im)material forms that have existed in economic history.

A critical appraisal of the history of economic thought is also necessary to understand the specific role of banks in a monetary economy of production. This is also instrumental in helping to prevent banks from exploiting their money issuance capacity to inflate a series of credit bubbles whose bursting elicits a systemic crisis (such as the global financial crisis that erupted in 2008). Understanding the fact that banks grant credit lines independently of pre-existent savings is particularly important for the design and implementation of those micro- and macroprudential policy tools that are intended to avoid the inflation of some other major credit bubbles and thereby the occurrence of another systemic crisis around the world. The mainstream view of money and banking, which informs current political choices and so-called 'unconventional' monetary policy interventions, must be rejected on both logical and conceptual grounds, making use of the history of economic thought to explain that banks are special because they issue money and provide credit without the need for them to dispose of pre-existent savings. As such, banking regulations must be considered anew, since the current regulatory framework is flawed by an essentially wrong conception of money and banking. Similarly, central bank interventions must be rethought entirely, considering the scriptural nature of money and its endogenous origin, as banks issue it independently of the actual monetary policy stance. Neither 'helicopter money' (Friedman, 1969, pp. 4–5) nor negative rates of interest can induce banks again to provide credit lines to non-financial firms, as imagined by their proponents to dispose of the negative consequences of a major financial crisis, unless the fiscal policy stance supports economic growth and job creation by increasing public expenditures, thereby inducing both firms and households to increase their own investment and consumption expenditures in a virtuous circle for the economy as a whole over the long run.

Teachers of economics have a crucial role to play if they want to contribute to avoiding the next major financial crisis. First of all, however, they must be aware of this role, as well as of the peculiar nature of money and banking. Let us hope that this chapter has rung a bell in their minds, before the alarm sets off noisily to signal the manifestation of another systemic crisis, whose ultimate origin lies in the current economics mainstream (see Caballero, 2010).

NOTES

1. In reality, from a neoclassical perspective, money can be omitted from the analysis in first-year courses. For instance, economic analysis is carried out by means of exchange and Edgeworth boxes where there is no money. Aggregate demand and supply analysis, production functions, production possibility frontiers all omit money from their analysis. If money is introduced in neoclassical models, it is done later, and is claimed that it makes exchange easier but it is not vital to the analysis.
2. For instance, this is the reason the discussion of money and the banking system appears in the very first chapters of Rochon and Rossi's (2016) introductory macroeconomics textbook.

REFERENCES

Bailly, J.-L., A. Cencini and S. Rossi (eds) (2017), *Quantum Macroeconomics: The Legacy of Bernard Schmitt*, London and New York: Routledge.
Bofinger, P. (2001), *Monetary Policy: Goals, Institutions, Strategies, and Instruments*, Oxford: Oxford University Press.

Caballero, R.J. (2010), 'Macroeconomics after the crisis: Time to deal with the pretense-of-knowledge syndrome', *Journal of Economic Perspectives*, **24**(4), 85–102.

Cardim de Carvalho, F.J. (2015), 'Basel agreements', in L.-P. Rochon and S. Rossi (eds), *The Encyclopedia of Central Banking*, Cheltenham, UK and Northampton, MA, USA: Edward Elgar Publishing, pp. 48–50.

Cencini, A. (2003), 'IS–LM: A final rejection', in L.-P. Rochon and S. Rossi (eds), *Modern Theories of Money: The Nature and Role of Money in Capitalist Economies*, Cheltenham, UK and Northampton, MA, USA: Edward Elgar Publishing, pp. 295–321.

Cencini, A. (2005), *Macroeconomic Foundations of Macroeconomics*, London and New York: Routledge.

Cencini, A. and S. Rossi (2015), *Economic and Financial Crises: A New Macroeconomic Analysis*, Basingstoke, UK and New York: Palgrave Macmillan.

Chick, V. (1986), 'The evolution of the banking system and the theory of saving, investment and interest', *Economies et Sociétés*, **20**(8–9), 111–26.

Chick, V. and S. Dow (2002), 'Monetary policy with endogenous money and liquidity preference: A nondualistic treatment', *Journal of Post Keynesian Economics*, **24**(4), 587–607.

Di Lorenzo, P. (2014), 'Insights on tax evasion using a monetary circuit model', *Metroeconomica*, **65**(1), 36–57.

Figuera, S. (2015), 'Banking and currency schools', in L.-P. Rochon and S. Rossi (eds), *The Encyclopedia of Central Banking*, Cheltenham, UK and Northampton, MA, USA: Edward Elgar Publishing, pp. 28–9.

Fisher, I. ([1911] 1931), *The Purchasing Power of Money: Its Determination and Relation to Credit, Interest and Crises*, New York: Macmillan.

Friedman, M. (1969), *The Optimum Quantity of Money and Other Essays*, Chicago, IL: Aldine Publishing.

Friedman, M. (1974), 'A theoretical framework for monetary analysis', in R.J. Gordon (ed.), *Milton Friedman's Monetary Framework: A Debate with His Critics*, Chicago, IL: University of Chicago Press, pp. 1–62.

Friedman, M. (1987), 'Quantity theory of money', in J. Eatwell, M. Milgate and P. Newman (eds), *The New Palgrave: A Dictionary of Economics, Vol. 4*, London and Basingstoke: Macmillan, pp. 3–20.

Fullarton, J. (1845), *On the Regulation of Currencies*, 2nd edition, New York: Augustus M. Kelley.

Goodhart, C.A.E. (1989), *Money, Information and Uncertainty*, 2nd edition, London: Macmillan.

Graziani, A. (1990), 'The theory of the monetary circuit', *Economies et Sociétés*, **24**(6), 7–36.

Graziani, A. (2003), *The Monetary Theory of Production*, Cambridge, UK: Cambridge University Press.

Hahn, F.H. (1973), 'On the foundations of monetary theory', in M. Parkin and A.R. Nobay (eds), *Essays in Modern Economics*, London: Longman, pp. 230–42.

106   *Teaching the history of economic thought*

Hayek, F.A. (1933), *Monetary Theory and the Trade Cycle*, London: Jonathan Cape.

Hicks, J.R. (1967), *Critical Essays in Monetary Theory*, Oxford: Clarendon Press.

Hume, D. ([1752] 1955), 'Of money', in E. Rotwein (ed.), *David Hume: Writings on Economics*, Edinburgh: Thomas Nelson and Sons, pp. 33–46.

Jevons, W.S. (1875), *Money and the Mechanism of Exchange*, London: Appleton.

Keynes, J.M. ([1933] 1973), 'The monetary theory of production', in G. Clausing (ed.), *Der Stand und die nächste Zukunft der Konjukturforschung: Festschrift für Arthur Spiethoff*, Munich: Duncker and Humblot, pp. 123–5. Reprinted in *The Collected Writings of John Maynard Keynes, Vol. XIII – The General Theory and After, Part I – Presentation*, D. Moggridge (ed.), London: Macmillan, pp. 408–11.

Keynes, J.M. (1936), *The General Theory of Employment, Interest and Money*, London: Macmillan.

Keynes, J.M. (1973), *The Collected Writings of John Maynard Keynes, Vol. XIII – The General Theory and After, Part I – Presentation*, D. Moggridge (ed.), London: Macmillan.

Knodell, J. (2017), 'Money endogeneity before central banking: Perspectives from monetary history', in L.-P. Rochon and S. Rossi (eds), *Advances in Endogenous Money Analysis*, Cheltenham, UK and Northampton, MA, USA: Edward Elgar Publishing, 21–49.

Lavoie, M. (1996), 'Monetary policy in an economy with endogenous credit money', in G. Deleplace and E.J. Nell (eds), *Money in Motion: The Post-Keynesian and Circulation Approaches*, Basingstoke, UK and New York: Macmillan and St. Martin's Press, pp. 532–45.

Lavoie, M. (1999), 'The credit-led supply of deposits and the demand for money: Kaldor's reflux mechanism as previously endorsed by Joan Robinson', *Cambridge Journal of Economics*, **23**(1), 103–13.

Lavoie, M. (2014), *Post-Keynesian Economics: New Foundations*, Cheltenham, UK and Northampton, MA, USA: Edward Elgar Publishing.

Massonnet, J. (2015), 'Natural rate of interest', in L.-P. Rochon and S. Rossi (eds), *The Encyclopedia of Central Banking*, Cheltenham, UK and Northampton, MA, USA: Edward Elgar Publishing, pp. 374–6.

Mihailov, A. (2015), 'Friedman rule', in L.-P. Rochon and S. Rossi (eds), *The Encyclopedia of Central Banking*, Cheltenham, UK and Northampton, MA, USA: Edward Elgar Publishing, pp. 219–22.

Parguez, A. and M. Seccareccia (2000), 'The credit theory of money: The monetary circuit approach', in J. Smithin (ed.), *What is Money?*, London and New York: Routledge, pp. 101–23.

Ricardo, D. ([1810–11] 2004), 'High price of bullion. A proof of the depreciation of bank notes', in P. Sraffa (ed.), *The Works and Correspondence of David Ricardo, Vol. 3*, Indianapolis, IN: Liberty Fund, pp. 47–127.

Robertson, D.H. (1937), *Money*, Cambridge, UK: Cambridge University Press.

Rochon, L.-P. (1999), *Credit, Money and Production: An Alternative Post-*

Keynesian Approach, Cheltenham, UK and Northampton, MA, USA: Edward Elgar Publishing.

Rochon, L.-P. and S. Rossi (2013), 'Endogenous money: The evolutionary versus revolutionary views', *Review of Keynesian Economics*, **1**(2), 210–29.

Rochon, L.-P. and S. Rossi (eds) (2016), *An Introduction to Macroeconomics: A Heterodox Approach to Economic Analysis*, Cheltenham, UK and Northampton, MA, USA: Edward Elgar Publishing.

Rochon, L.-P. and S. Rossi (eds) (2017), *Advances in Endogenous Money Analysis*, Cheltenham, UK and Northampton, MA, USA: Edward Elgar Publishing.

Rogers, C. (1989), *Money, Interest and Capital: A Study in the Foundations of Monetary Theory*, Cambridge, UK: Cambridge University Press.

Rossi, S. (2007), *Money and Payments in Theory and Practice*, London and New York: Routledge.

Rossi, S. (2011), 'Can it happen again? Structural policies to avert further systemic crises', *International Journal of Political Economy*, **40**(2), 61–78.

Rossi, S. (2012), 'The fundamental role of money and banking in macroeconomic analysis and policymaking', *International Journal of Pluralism and Economics Education*, **3**(3), 308–19.

Rossi, S. (forthcoming), 'Milton Friedman and the monetarist school', in H. Bougrine and L.-P. Rochon (eds), *A Brief History of Economic Thought: An Introduction to Alternative Schools and Their Development*, Cheltenham, UK and Northampton, MA, USA: Edward Elgar Publishing.

Schumpeter, J.A. (1954), *History of Economic Analysis*, London: George Allen & Unwin.

Servet, J.-M. (1994), 'La fable du troc', *Dix-huitième Siècle*, **26**(1), 103–15.

Smith, A. ([1776] 1991), *An Inquiry into the Nature and Causes of the Wealth of Nations*, Oxford: Clarendon Press.

Tooke, T. (1844), *An Inquiry into the Currency Principle*, London: Longmans, Brown, Green & Longmans.

Torrens, R. (1837), *A Letter on the Causes of the Recent Derangement in the Money Market and on Bank Reform*, London: Longmans, Brown, Green & Longmans.

Walker, F.A. (1880), *Money in its Relations to Trade and Industry*, London: Macmillan.

Woodford, M. (2003), *Interest and Prices: Foundations of a Theory of Monetary Policy*, Princeton, NJ and Oxford: Princeton University Press.

8. Teaching financial economics with historical perspectives

Luigi Ventimiglia

1 INTRODUCTION

When I joined the School of Economics and Finance (SEF) at Queen Mary University of London (QMUL) in 2013, the head of school asked me to take on a core second- and third-year finance module of 200 students. This module provides the theoretical framework for financial theories and allows students to move into more applicative modules in the third year. During my first year at QMUL, I realized that the module lacked a logical flow, since the teaching material and the related textbook, which had been used for some time, addressed financial theories with no clear explanation of how they came about or any analysis of the underlying assumptions that might have helped students to locate the various models within any particular school of thought. After a number of discussions with various colleagues, I thought that this logical flow could be provided by introducing a historical narrative that would work as an overarching narrative linking the different topics, theories and models. With this idea in mind, I decided to restructure the module. Subsequently, in cooperation with other colleagues and as a result of the reflective activity I undertook during my studies for the Postgraduate Certificate in Academic Practice (PGCAP), I contributed to fine-tune this approach, giving it the name of 'teaching with historical perspectives' (THP).

This chapter shows how THP is about contextualizing the teaching of a subject both in terms of the genesis of a model or theory, and in terms of its development and evolution. THP provides a framework that allows students to group models together within the same school of thought and discuss the formation of new paradigms.

As a result, students are also exposed to pluralism: they are encouraged to reflect on how the discipline has evolved as a result of debates around the assumptions of a particular model/theory. For this reason, it is crucial to tease out the assumptions that underlie each model and what effects these have on its results and applications.

The chapter is divided into two further sections. In section 2, following this introduction, five examples are presented (in subsections 2.1 to 2.5) to illustrate how THP can be used in teaching financial economics. The first example illustrates how THP can help in contextualizing the genesis of a model and to introduce pluralism. The second concentrates on an in-depth analysis of a model considering the *evolution* of its applications in real financial practice. The third example builds on the previous two and shows how THP can provide helpful support in explaining the evolution of a model/theory, while the fourth discusses how THP can help in locating various models within the same or competing schools of thought. Last, drawing on the previous ones, especially on the analysis of the assumptions, the fifth example shows how to contextualize different models within the same school of thought.

Section 3 of the chapter looks at the reaction of students to the redesigned module with the aim of discovering whether they have found THP to be helpful and stimulating. The hope is that THP will become a method of study that can be applied to other modules.

2 THE IMPACT OF THP IN REDESIGNING THE MODULE

This section of the chapter presents five different examples of how THP can be implemented. The sequence of the examples is determined by the increasing complexity of the teaching objective/learning outcome.

2.1 Example 1: Introducing Finance

This first example is taken from the first lecture of the module and is intended to complement the standard introduction used by mainstream textbooks. Once THP has embedded the idea of pluralism in teaching, students familiarize with the existence of different approaches. These approaches are usually new to them, since students tend to recognize different theories just as given, and not in relation to various schools of thought, each of which may build on different assumptions or have different focuses and objectives.

Mainstream introductory financial economics textbooks tend to be divided into two main parts, the first of which explains how financial markets work and describes the industry, its agents and its financial instruments, while the second focuses on the principles of portfolio construction and the different models used to price securities and their returns. However, the first part displays some important deficiencies: there is a clear lack of any evolution in financial theory. For example, there is no indication of how financial markets have actually developed, how institutions have evolved into their current form, and, most notably, there is no discussion about the relation of finance with the real economy, nor any mention of one of the phenomena frequently debated in recent years – financialization as a historically specific phenomenon. Thus, within this module's introduction, two basic concepts need to be presented to complement any mainstream textbook.

First, students need to acknowledge how financial markets have gained a predominant role in society. Of course, students may recognize that financialization is the main reason they want to study finance! 'Financialization means the increasing role of financial motives, financial markets, financial actors and financial institutions in the operation of the domestic and international economies' (Epstein, 2005, p. 3). Recent data illustrate the increase in the profits of financial corporations relative to non-financial corporations, the share of economic growth relative to the other sectors of the economy, the increase in non-tangible assets relative to tangible assets, increased wage inequality between the financial and non-financial sectors, and the creation of the students' loan market.

Second, students are exposed to the existence of competing theories about the players in the markets and how they behave. For example, in mainstream textbooks, banks are considered important agents, acting as intermediaries that transform short-term liabilities, such as households' deposits, into medium- or long-term assets, such as loans to firms. Students can then be exposed to Keynes and to how, after his death, competing interpretations and adaptations of his theory emerged, such as the neoclassical synthesis and the post-Keynesian school of thought. In contrast to the neoclassical synthesis, for post-Keynesians (Lavoie, 1999): 'One common misconception is that banks act simply as intermediaries, lending out deposits that savers place with them. In this view, deposits are typically "created" by the saving decisions of households and banks "lend" out those existing deposits to borrowers' (McLeay, Radia and Thoms, 2014, pp. 15–16). 'Commercial banks create money, in the form of bank deposits, by making new loans' (ibid.).

From the very first lecture, THP can provide an excellent pedagogical tool by introducing students to the idea of the evolution of the discipline and, from this, to pluralism. The next example focuses on the more complex issue of a class discussion around a financial model.

2.2   Example 2: The Markowitz Model

This section shows an example of how to use THP in discussing a model. In doing so, not only can we tease out the underlying assumptions of the model and place it in its historical context, we can also focus on a specific conceptualization of one of its basic principles – risk and uncertainty.

Usually, the first lectures of a mainstream finance module focus on describing the return of an asset and its statistical distribution in order to introduce the so-called 'modern portfolio theory'. The expected return of an asset is calculated as the mean of its historical returns, and its associated risk is specified by their variance. Within THP, students grasp that during the 1950s, modern probability theory was applied for the first time to financial markets and corporate finance. Within this framework, the mean–variance theory is related to the work of Markowitz (1952). This model is centred on the assumption that returns are approximately normally distributed; thus, an investor has sufficient information on any asset by considering only the first two moments of the distribution, mean and variance. Therefore, if investors are rational and know the future distribution of assets, they are able to make optimal decisions.

Students are encouraged to historically contextualize this model: the neoclassical synthesis emerged as an adaptation of Keynes's original thought to the theoretical scaffolding of neoclassical economics.[1] In parallel, mainstream finance laid down its foundations by incorporating an astonishingly simple assumption about human knowledge of risk that Keynes had explicitly dismissed: 'There is no scientific basis on which to form any calculable probability whatever... We simply do not know' (Keynes, 1973, p. 214). Keynes debated that the future is unknowable and uncertain. In practice, mainstream finance substituted the word 'risk' for 'uncertainty', overturning Keynes's understanding of the nature of financial markets.

The consequences of the mainstream assumptions and stylization are straightforward and mathematically neat. Markowitz provides a technique that allows the construction of a portfolio of assets as part of the solution to an optimization problem, in which the only inputs required are the means and variances of historical distributions. The aim is to obtain a portfolio with minimum variance holding constant expected return, the so-called minimum variance portfolio. By identifying the efficient frontier formed by all those portfolios that provide higher returns for higher risk, investors can choose a particular portfolio depending on their individual risk–return preferences. Markowitz allows investors to validate the intuition that correlation between assets is crucial in constructing a portfolio, and this reveals the advantages of diversification in terms of risk reduction. The application of the model is relevant for students' employability because all practitioners study mainstream finance, and their daily operations are influenced by their studies. The opportunity set derived from the combination of different assets and portfolio diversification is a notion still used today.

Once students learn the model in terms of assumptions and results, they are able to reflect on how realistic it is. First, can we realistically approximate returns as normally distributed? The Chief Financial Officer of Goldman Sachs at the time of the crisis, David Viniar, may help students to answer this question. In August 2007, he declared that Goldman's flagship GEO hedge fund had lost 27 per cent of its value since the start of the year, and explained the reasons: 'We were seeing things that were 25 standard-deviation moves, several days in a row' (*Financial Times*, 2007). Just to give a sense of the meaning of this distribution, Dowd et al. (2008) have calculated that an eight standard-deviation event has a probability of occurring once since the Big Bang. This example elucidates how return distribution can radically change during periods of turmoil. As a consequence, measures of portfolio risk based on an assumption of normality are, in reality, flawed. Second, not only exceptional events, especially negative ones, are more likely than the prediction based on normal distribution; also, variances and co-variances increase in turbulent times. So, portfolio diversifications cease to spread the risk when extreme negative events happen during a period of turmoil.

Third, as pointed out in the cross-asset report published by J.P. Morgan (Sheikh and Qiao, 2009), for the model to be applicable, investors would have to estimate a large number of variables: the expected returns and variances for each asset, and, most significantly, all the covariances for all pairs of assets. Just to provide an example for students, if we wanted to calculate the minimum variance portfolio composed by the 3000 equity firms of the New York Stock Exchange, we would have to run 4.5 million estimations. This clearly shows that the estimation can lead to the wrong results.

These are just three of the flaws in the Markowitz conceptualization of risk that have recently been discussed, and that many scholars consider to undermine the very core of the foundations of modern finance.

At this stage, students have reflected on how the historical context can be useful in identifying the development of a model. This is determined by its assumptions, which might affect not only its theoretical limitations but also its realism and actual applicability. The historical perspective also allows us to provide an interpretation of how the model has been used since its creation, and its influence on the practice of portfolio management since then. The next example shows how THP can be helpful in the transition from one model to another.

2.3   Example 3: From Markowitz to the CAPM

This example shows how two different models can be linked by adopting the THP framework. In most mainstream finance modules, the second model that students study after Markowitz is the capital asset pricing model (CAPM) developed in the 1960s. In this example, THP allows students to understand the development of finance theory during the 1960s, showing in general how new models arise as the result of debates that expose the limitations of older models. Therefore, in contrast with their experiences in previous modules, students are necessarily engaged in a reflective process in which critical thinking is vital: the assumptions and functioning of the various models are debated and various viewpoints and critiques are evaluated. The development of the Markowitz model might be introduced by the following anecdote. Markowitz developed his model as part of his PhD dissertation in economics at Chicago. During the PhD viva examination, Friedman raised the issue that Markowitz's portfolio theory was certainly interesting and well designed, but it wasn't economics: 'Harry, I don't see anything wrong with the math here, but I have a problem. This isn't a dissertation in economics, and we can't give you a PhD in economics for a dissertation that's not economics. It's not math, it's not economics, it's not even business administration' (Bernstein, 1992, p. 60).

This introduction illustrates how Friedman's positivism (1953) was a key element of the development of financial economics. He believed that a more complex model was needed, one that included more economics, so that, coherently and in a way that was similar to other parts of economics, investors' behaviour could be systematically approached. This new model had to overcome some of the clear limitations discussed in the previous section. In other words, by the 1950s, general equilibrium had become the foundation of microeconomics, so it had to be incorporated into finance too.

The CAPM served this purpose. Developed by Sharpe (1964), Lintner (1965) and Mossin (1966), this model determines the equilibrium price for an asset, given its risk, and whether the market acts as a mechanism for pricing securities correctly. The model was supposed to provide a benchmark rate of return for evaluating possible investments and to assist investors in making an informed guess about the expected return of securities that had not yet been traded in the marketplace. Thus, the CAPM involves asset pricing, portfolio construction theory and aggregate implications of individual investors' behaviour using the concept of equilibrium: prices are determined by aggregate supply and aggregate demand, which is affected by the optimal portfolio selection of investors, given market prices. Thus, investors' choices and market prices are determined *simultaneously* according to the functioning of general equilibrium. Moreover, portfolio theory can be seen as a form of partial equilibrium analysis: it is possible to work out the individual investors' optimal portfolio selection because prices are taken as fixed and investors do not affect prices.

Once students have grasped the original idea of the CAPM and its relation to general equilibrium they can then be persuaded to think in terms of a system of thought, given the aim of the model and its assumptions, which can be divided into two sets. The first set is about the functioning of capital markets: there are many investors, each with an endowment that is small compared to the total endowments of all investors. They do not interact with each other directly; their interaction occurs only through the anonymous auctioneer. Investors are price takers, meaning that security prices are unaffected by their own trades. As a consequence, investments must be limited to a universe of publicly traded financial securities such as stocks and bonds, and to risk-free (e.g., Treasury Bills) borrowing or lending arrangements. Moreover, it is assumed that investors may lend or borrow any amount at a fixed risk-free rate. For simplicity, they do not pay taxes on returns or transaction costs (service and commissions charges) on trades in assets. Markets are frictionless, thus liquidity is not an issue and there is perfect information. After discussing this set of assumptions, students may find many similarities with other modules they have studied, and realize that there is common ground underlying these ideas (i.e., mainstream microfoundations). This possibility is tested in the survey discussed in section 3.

The second set of assumptions defines investors' behaviour. For simplicity, their behaviour is considered myopic, in the sense that they disregard everything that might happen after the end of the single period in which they invest. All investors are rational and they use the mean variance portfolio selection Markowitz model. They have homogeneous expectations and beliefs, and they analyse securities in the same way, sharing the same economic view of the world (mathematically, they have the same estimation of probability distributions). Consequently, given the prices, the risk-free rate and different securities, they use the same expected returns and variance and covariance between security returns to generate the best possible portfolios following the Markowitz model. After discussing this second set of assumptions, students become aware that this model is 'just a model'. However, it is worth pointing out that, as far as realism is concerned, even Sharpe was well aware of the problem:

> Needless to say, these are highly restrictive and undoubtedly unrealistic assumptions. However, since the proper test of a theory is not the realism of its assumptions but the acceptability of its implications, and since these assumptions imply equilibrium conditions which form a major part of classical financial doctrine, it is far from clear that this formulation should be rejected. (Sharpe, 1964, p. 434)

This quote first encourages students to reflect on the lack of realism of the model, a problem from which mainstream models often suffer, and, second, it paves the way to an additional consideration: the overall result of the CAPM model is that every investor holds a portfolio of risky assets in shares equal to those assets in the market portfolio (by definition the market portfolio includes all traded assets). Thus, the market portfolio lies on the efficient frontier and corresponds with the optimal risky portfolio. Moreover, the risk premium on individual assets is proportional to the risk premium on the market portfolio multiplied by its beta (beta measures the extent to which returns on the stock and the market move together). In relation to risk, the necessity of introducing the idea of equilibrium into the working of capital markets narrows the focus on the undiversifiable risk: the only risk that counts is the systematic risk of an asset or a portfolio. For this reason, then, the CAPM overcomes what was perceived as a limitation of the Markowitz model: in order to calculate the expected return of a portfolio, investors no longer need to estimate the covariance of all possible pairs of assets, but only the covariance of each asset relative to the market. This diminishes dramatically the number of estimations, and thus the likelihood of error.

THP approaches this evolution of financial theory in terms of its historical impact on financial practice. The practical consequence of the CAPM is that investors can obtain their desired portfolio by mixing the market portfolio with a risk-free asset. Consequently, there is no need to seek extra returns in excess of the market returns because with a well-diversified portfolio the only residual risk is the market/systematic risk. This conclusion was crucial for the development of the passive-fund management industry. Passive funds, which developed with the privatization of pension funds after the 1970s, simply replicate indexes and are not supposed to take any extra risk for additional performance. In this case the academic world and the financial industry created a mutually beneficial relationship in developing theories and in justifying the expansion of the financial industry. This link will be reconsidered later in the module.

Once the theoretical development of the CAPM model, the consequences for the money manager industry, and its link with academia are introduced, the THP framework allows for smooth progress towards the development of the next model at the end of the 1960s (Sharpe, 1967), the single-index model, which operationalizes the applicability of the CAPM. This is a model that, with some variations, is still used today by some financial institutions for risk management.

The next example will show how THP not only provides a useful framework for migrating teaching-wise from one model to the next, but it also allows for locating models within specific schools of thoughts and for reflection on how new paradigms emerge.

2.4   Example 4: The Establishment of a New Paradigm

This subsection shows how THP can group more models within the same school of thought, allowing students to identify new paradigms developed during specific periods.

The exposure of students to the economics underpinning financial theory, as detailed in the previous examples, easily introduces a new paradigm based on the efficient market hypothesis (EMH). Once students are familiar with the assumptions of the CAPM, they become more confident in attempting a discussion about the developments in financial theory in the 1960s.

The origins of the formulation of the EMH are found in earlier works in which the aim of the research was the econometric study of market prices: for example, Cowles (1933) and Kendall (1953) attempted to explain the random character of the stock market. In search of a theory that could explain the random pattern of prices, Working (1956) recognized the first explicit relation between the unpredictability of new information and the random walk of stocks. Only in 1960 did Cowles make the first reference to a competitive market in equilibrium. From the THP point of view, it is important that students contextualize this historically within the evolution of the discipline in relation to the development of its technical apparatus: it was only in the 1960s that the mathematical treatment of the random character of the stock market became standard practice for mainstream finance (Cootner, 1964).

These are the foundations of the EMH, which were first formulated in Fama's PhD thesis in 1964: 'A market in which prices always "fully reflect" available information is called "efficient"' (Fama, 1970, p. 383). Then, theoretical explanations based on economic theories were formulated establishing financial economics (Jovanovic, 2008).

Within this new paradigm, the relation between the assumption of rationality and the uncertain character of the financial markets took on a particular shape: in a competitive market, random prices are not due to irrationality, they are, in fact, the consequence of rational investors competing in discovering new information. In this environment, investors have a (competitive) advantage that is determined by how much sooner than other investors they acquire a new set of information. Nevertheless, given the unpredictable nature of new information, prices are unpredictable; predictability in prices would imply market inefficiencies. At equilibrium, competition among analysts should ensure that asset prices reflect the available information about their fair levels, for otherwise there might be arbitrage opportunities. As a consequence, it is not possible to use past information to predict present and future prices; the random walk simply represents the dynamic evolution of such equilibrium prices.

Students usually have little difficulty in becoming mechanically familiar with the various versions of the EMH. However, they need some guidance when the focus shifts to its implications, which are of two types, and here again THP can be very helpful. First, with the establishment of EMH literature has come a development of various techniques aimed at proving the random character of the stock market, which would verify the EMH. Looking at a series of empirical studies, students may realize that the development of financial economics as a subdiscipline and the community of researchers associated with it were effectively established in the 1960s with the appearance not only of books and collections of articles, but also of articles in journals such as the *Journal of Finance* and the *Journal of Financial and Quantitative Analysis*. A specific terminology related to this new stream of research developed. A specialized journal on the subject, the *Journal of Financial Economics*, was first published in 1974.

Second, the EMH has generated a series of fierce debates both in academia and between professionals. This aspect will be the focus of the last example.

2.5   Example 5: The Creation of the School of Thought

This last example shows how THP is used to contextualize different models within the same school of thought. Once this has been established, THP can also show how the development of debates and critiques may create alternative views, and, therefore, different schools of thought.

Once students have realized how the development of financial theory has also evolved in relation to what the new research methods and econometric techniques have allowed it to do, they can appreciate that researchers have moved in two main directions since the 1970s: either they have created new models, or they have tried to improve the CAPM model by relaxing the unrealistic assumptions that led to its failure in empirical testing.

A well-known model born out of a critique of the CAPM is the arbitrage pricing theory (APT) model. The issues identified by the failure of the empirical testing of the CAPM led to speculation that the CAPM may not be a complete description of the expected risk–return relation, because of missing variables that influence expected returns. Still, under the condition of having a sufficient number of securities to diversify away idiosyncratic risk, adding additional factors entails having a less structured model, which could freely incorporate other sources of risk. Ross (1976) developed the APT, which required fewer assumptions than the CAPM. Most importantly, APT makes no assumptions about the empirical distribution of security returns, and there is no special role for the market portfolio because any well-diversified portfolio may serve as the benchmark portfolio. Besides, APT can be enhanced into a model that incorporates more than one factor of risk.

The APT is based on arbitrage that occurs if there is zero or little risk (investment) with a sure profit; and it is based on the law of one price, which states that if two assets are equivalent in all economically relevant respects, then they should have the same market price, otherwise there is an arbitrage opportunity. In this environment, the law of one price is enforced by arbitrageurs, who are responsible for market efficiency. Therefore, well-functioning markets do not allow for persistence of arbitrage. Also, the ATP model is still based on equilibrium, but while in the CAPM model if a security is mispriced all investors trade a small amount of that security, tilting the same mean variance efficient portfolios and returning the price of that security to equilibrium, here a few investors, the arbitrageurs, who identify the arbitrage opportunity, trade as much as possible, given that there is no or little risk associated with the arbitrage trade.

The comparison between the CAPM and the APT is a brilliant example for class discussion on how different assumptions within the same equilibrium paradigm and market efficiency can lead to different results. Besides, in terms of the evolution of the discipline, the development of research methods, namely econometric techniques, which became possible with the increased power of computers between the 1970s and the 1980s, influenced the direction of research at the expense of alternative theories. In this case, multifactor models, which rely on obtaining information directly from large data sets, are able to capture sources of risk other than the market, but provide less guidance in terms of meaning and the magnitude of the different factors of risk. In terms of skills to be acquired, multifactor models are still used in the industry today to design trading models, which provide measures of over- or undervaluations and possible sources of risk for portfolios. In this respect, the work of Chen, Roll and Ross (1986) and Fama and French (1993) has to be presented in class.

Beside the APT, an alternative critique was developed in the 1970s. Within the assumptions of all equilibrium models described above, two sets of assumptions are crucial: one relates to the functioning of the market and the EMH; the other is a behavioural assumption relative to investors' rationality. Referring to the latter, alternative hypotheses of irrationality have been collected under the subdiscipline of behavioural finance (BF) since the development of prospect theory (Kahneman and Tversky, 1979), which defined different utility functions, depending on possible gains or losses of wealth of investors. As stated by BF, agents either fail to update their beliefs correctly or have a behavioural bias that affects their decision. Consequently, asset prices may deviate from fundamental values and not come back to equilibrium for a long time, so strategies to correct mispricing can be risky and costly, limiting the possibility of arbitraging. BF represents an example of a multidisciplinary approach in which cognitive psychology has provided a new dimension to the research. This is a brilliant example of an alternative theory that has been so successful that it has now been included in standard mainstream textbooks. The ascendance of BF has been well received by practitioners who never fully accepted the EMH.

By this stage, students have acquired a set of skills aimed at developing their critical thinking, and they have a good understanding of the historical evolution of financial economics. Students have learned that a model output will vary depending on its assumptions. Probably for the first time since they started to study economics, they have become familiar with the unsettling idea that for some issues, like market efficiency, there may be more than one solution (or answer). The final leap consists of looking at the history of the discipline and framing what has been learned in terms of schools of thought.

Students can appreciate that mainstream financial theories come mainly from the Chicago School of thought, also named the 'freshwater school' on account of its location around the Great Lakes

(Kilborn, 1988), formed by Friedman, Markowitz, Fisher, Sharpe, Miller, Fama, Jensen and Lucas. In Chicago, the Center for Research and Security Prices (CRSP) today still provides data and analysis of securities. The other celebrated fathers of financial economics, Black and Scholes, directed the centre for many years. A significant role was played by the financial industry (e.g., Pearce and Merrill Lynch), which provided grants for CRSP, funding the expansion of the theoretical and academic justification for the increasing size of finance in the economy. This school of thought is based on mathematical internal consistency rather than empirical validity. The theory, centred on rational individuals, had great expectations of the role of free markets, and the school promoted laissez-faire principles and deregulation of the financial industry. Some authors use the term 'economic imperialism' when writing about Chicago, since 'for half a century, Chicago's hands-off principles have permeated financial thinking and shaped global markets, earning the university 10 memorial prizes in Economic Sciences starting in 1969, more than double the four each won by Columbia University, Harvard University, Princeton University and the University of California, Berkeley' (Lippert, 2008).

On the contrary, but still mainstream in terms of econometric methodology, the literature that focuses on critiques of the EMH and is generally supportive of government intervention, derives from the MIT School of thought, named the 'saltwater school' owing to MIT's proximity to the sea. Since the 1960s, MIT (Cootner, Samuelson and Steiger, for example) has emphasized the random character of stock market prices, contending against Chicago that markets are not efficient. Researchers belonging to this school also include Stiglitz, Greenspan and Krugman.

Today, in the aftermath of the 2008 financial crisis, the two schools of thought still provide their visions on the interpretation of events, and practitioners still debate on the extent to which the EMH is realistic: 'On a deeper level, the demise of Lehman Brothers conclusively falsifies the efficient market hypothesis' (Soros, 2009, p. 65):

> Among financial economists, Keynes's disparaging vision of financial markets as a 'casino' was replaced by 'efficient market' theory, which asserted that financial markets always get asset prices right given the available information... Discussion of investor irrationality, of bubbles, of destructive speculation had virtually disappeared from academic discourse... In short, the belief in efficient financial markets blinded

many if not most economists to the emergence of the biggest financial bubble in history. (Krugman, 2009)

3   EVALUATING THE NEW TEACHING APPROACH

This second part of the chapter focuses on the evaluation of THP over two academic years, 2015/16 and 2016/17.

3.1   The Method

In order to evaluate the redesign of the module, I used a mixed-method approach combining a short online survey with a series of semi-structured interviews.

The anonymous online survey was designed to provide an initial measure of the success of the teaching method and an evaluation of the impact of the method. Students were asked to respond to the survey just after the last week of teaching of the year 2016/17, after they had experienced the entire module. The survey was carried out online following an email invitation. The number of students who responded was 81. Each cohort is of about 170 students; however, the average attendance for the module is about 85 per cent, meaning that, realistically, over the two years it is fair to assume a real number of 300 students engaging with the method. Therefore, the response rate has been about 28 per cent, presumably skewed towards the last cohort. The survey included nine questions: two in which students were asked to respond to a question or statement by giving a rating on a scale of 1 to 10, one open question and six multiple choice questions.

Students were also invited via email to participate in an interview, conducted in the absence of the lecturer. Five students participated from the 2015/16 cohort and nine students from the 2016/17 cohort. The main scope of the interviews was to investigate some of the responses obtained from the survey.

3.2   Results

The result of the rating questions of the survey is summarized in Table 8.1 at the end of the chapter. The two rating questions were aimed at investigating whether the historical approach was well received and whether students felt that they were exposed to pluralism:

Question 1   How helpful was the use of a historical/evolutionary approach in understanding the different models of capital markets – e.g., the Markowitz model (Markowitz, 1952); CAPM (Sharpe, 1964); APT (Ross, 1976)? (Answer question on a scale of 1 [not helpful] to 10 [very helpful].)

Question 2   The approach taken to teaching capital markets encourages pluralism (i.e., the theory that more than one system of thought might be considered valid). (Assess statement on a scale of 1 [disagree] to 10 [agree].)

The responses to question 1 showed that the historical approach was helpful (average score 6.90, and most of the responses at 8), and the responses to question 2 revealed that students had a clear perception that the module encouraged pluralism (average score 7.44, and most of the responses at 8).

The responses to the multiple choice questions are summarized in Table 8.2 at the end of the chapter. The six questions were as follows:

Question 3   Did this module help you make sense of your other economics modules?

Question 4   Do you think that by studying each model through its assumptions, empirical testing, applications and its critique you developed a methodology and a critical approach?

Question 5   Would you like more exposure to alternative economic and financial theories in your education?

Question 6   Has the historical and critical approach of this module made you think about selecting the history of economic thought module?

Question 7   Do you think that an exposure to different approaches to theories can better foster your skills and your employability?

Question 8   When did you first become aware of the existence of a historical evolution of the financial models?

Questions 3, 4 and 5 received 'yes' responses from around 90 per cent of respondents. This highlighted the fact that students liked the critical approach adopted by scrutinizing the assumptions of the models and verifying their applicability, and that they are interested

Table 8.1   Rating questions: number of responses by question and percentage

	1	2	3	4	5
Question 1 (Not helpful = 1; Very helpful = 10)	3 (3.70%)	0 (0.00%)	5 (6.17%)	3 (3.70%)	8 (9.88%)
Question 2 (Disagree =1; Agree = 10)	1 (1.23%)	1 (1.23%)	1 (1.23%)	1 (1.23%)	8 (9.88%)

in alternative theories. As one student confirmed in the interview: 'Studying different models was definitely helpful and refreshing for real-world use and application (rather than only one model that is taught as mathematical fact with no alternative approaches)' (Student 2). From another interview, we gathered a similar answer: 'Alternatives to unrealistic features like utility maximization would be welcome' (Student 5).

Students also found the approach helpful in understanding other modules, as they began to link school of thoughts to other subdisciplines. From the interviews, this aspect was highlighted: 'I realized that financial economics was developing along the lines of other parts of economics, like microeconomics and macroeconomics. I have never put things together in this way before!' (Student 3). This result was confirmed by the responses to Question 7, which proved that the pluralist and historical approach, in the way it was presented in the module, was particular attractive in terms of developing skills for employability, especially critical thinking and the ability to debate.

However, Question 6 produced a surprising result, with most of the students (about 75 per cent) declaring that they would rather not take the history of economic thought module, which is an optional module for third-year students, despite having liked the approach used in my module. Linking this to the response to Question 7, in the course of the interviews it became clear that the main reason behind this choice was that the module was considered too theoretical, and students were concerned about the impact of

6	7	8	9	10	Total	Weighted Average
11	13	19	10	9	81	6.90
(13.58%)	(16.05%)	(23.46%)	(12.35%)	(11.11%)	(100%)	
10	16	18	13	12	81	7.44
(12.35%)	(19.75%)	(22.22%)	(16.05%)	(14.81%)	(100%)	

a lack of practical skills on employability. In fact, most of the students who take my module are interested in finance and obtaining a job in the financial sector. So, the conclusion is that students liked the approach, but they need to see its benefit in practical terms. This feedback was passed to the module convenor of the history of economic thought module.

Finally, the last two questions focused on whether THP was a new approach for students. From Question 8 it emerged that it was new for about 50 per cent of the class while another 30 per cent had experienced it in the first year. The last question was an open question asking students to name which module they have studied with a historical perspective. It came out that only a couple of modules up to the end of the second year had some historical contextualization (games and strategies; macroeconomics). This finding was confirmed in the interviews.

4   CONCLUSION

This chapter discusses the teaching and learning experience of using THP in a financial module. In doing so, it illustrates five examples progressively increasing in complexity.

The results of the redesign of the module in terms of students' satisfaction have been positive. This outcome is clear both from teaching evaluation and from the student survey based on the last two academic years, 2015/16 and 2016/17. Students found the

Table 8.2   Multiple choice questions: number of responses by question and percentage

	Answer Choices	Responses	Percentage
Question 3	Yes	74	91.4%
	No	7	8.6%
	Total	81	100%
Question 4	Yes	76	93.8%
	No	5	6.2%
	Total	81	100%
Question 5	Yes	69	85.2%
	No	12	14.8%
	Total	81	100%
Question 6	Yes	19	23.5%
	No	62	76.5%
	Total	81	100%
Question 7	Yes	72	88.9%
	No	9	11.1%
	Total	81	100%
Question 8	Before university	13	16.0%
	During Capital Markets	41	50.6%
	During the first year	26	32.1%
	I am not aware of this	1	1.2%
Total		81	100%

module to be valuable, both in theoretical terms and in terms of the skills it fosters. The methodology has clearly been appreciated, despite the fact that undergraduate students who decide to take a finance module in a mainstream institution are primarily concerned with learning practical skills and techniques that will enhance their employability. By constantly being referred to reality, and its evolution throughout historical examples, students have developed a willingness to investigate alternative theories. In this respect, financial instability and crisis are useful in uncovering weaknesses in the mainstream model.

Overall, students have been given an exposure to the methods of inquiry typical of heterodox economists and pluralism. Even though the module is based on mainstream finance, students are made aware of alternative theories that have as a starting point the inclusion of realistic assumptions. For instance, they learn that post-Keynesians see markets as unstable.

NOTE

1. Often, according to the post-Keynesian school of thought, the neoclassical synthesis has operated a complete misinterpretation of Keynes.

REFERENCES

Bernstein, P.L. (1992), *Capital Ideas: The Improbable Origins of Modern Wall Street*, New York: Free Press.

Chen, N., R. Roll and S. Ross (1986), 'Economic forces and the stock market', *Journal of Business*, **59**(3), 383–403.

Cootner, P.H. (1964), *The Random Character of Stock Market Prices*, Cambridge, MA: MIT Press.

Cowles, A. (1933), 'Can stock market forecasters forecast?', *Econometrica*, **1**(3), 309–24.

Cowles, A. (1960), 'A revision of previous conclusions regarding stock price behavior', *Econometrica*, **28**(4), 909–15.

Dowd, K., J. Cotter, C. Humphrey and M. Woods (2008), 'How unlucky is 25-sigma?', *arXiv preprint*, accessed 10 April 2017 at http://arxiv.org/ftp/arxiv/papers/1103/1103.5672.pdf.

Epstein, G.A. (2005), *Financialization and the World Economy*, Cheltenham, UK and Northampton, MA, USA: Edward Elgar Publishing.

Fama, E.F. (1970), 'Efficient capital market: A review of theory and empirical work', *Journal of Finance*, **25**(2), 383–417.

Fama, E.F. and K.R. French (1993), 'Common risk factors in the return on stocks and bonds', *Journal of Financial Economics*, **33**(1), 3–56.

Financial Times (2007), 'Goldman pays the price of being big', 14 August.

Friedman, M.C. (1953), *Essays in Positive Economics*, Chicago, IL: University of Chicago Press.

Jovanovic, F. (2008), 'The construction of the canonical history of financial economics', *History of Political Economy*, **40**(2), 213–42.

Kahneman, D. and A. Tversky (1979), 'Prospect theory: An analysis of decision under risk', *Econometrica*, **47**(2), 263–92.

Kendall, M.G. (1953), 'The analysis of economic time-series – Part 1: Prices', *Journal of the Royal Statistical Society*, **116**, 11–25.

Keynes, J.M. (1973), *The General Theory of Employment, Interest and Money*, London: Macmillan.

Kilborn, P.T. (1988), '"Fresh water" economists gain', *New York Times*, 23 July, accessed 17 December 2017 at http://www.nytimes.com/1988/07/23/business/fresh-water-economists-gain.html?pagewan ted¼all&src¼pm.

Krugman, P. (2009), 'How did economists get it so wrong?', *New York Times*, 6 September, accessed 17 December 2017 at http://www.nytimes.com/2009/09/06/magazine/06Economic-t.html?pagewanted¼all.

Lavoie, M. (1999), 'The credit-led supply of deposits and the demand for money: Kaldor's reflux mechanism as previously endorsed by Joan Robinson', *Cambridge Journal of Economics*, **23**(1), 103–13.

Lintner, J. (1965), 'Security prices, risk and maximal gains from diversification', *Journal of Finance*, **20**(4), 587–615.

Lippert, J. (2008), 'John Lippert on the Chicago School', *Bloomberg*, 23 December, accessed 17 December 2017 at http://delong.typepad.com/egregious_moderation/2008/12/john-lippert-on-the-chicago-school.html.

Markowitz, H. (1952), 'Portfolio selection', *Journal of Finance*, **7**(1), 77–91.

McLeay, M., A. Radia and R. Thoms (2014), 'Money creation in the modern economy', *Bank of England Quarterly Bulletin*, First Quarter, 15–16.

Mossin, J. (1966), 'Equilibrium in a capital asset market', *Econometrica*, **34**(4), 768–83.

Ross, S.A. (1976), 'Return, risk and arbitrage', in I. Friend and J. Bicksler (eds), *Risk and Return in Finance*, Cambridge, MA: Ballinger, 189–218.

Sharpe, W.F. (1964), 'Capital asset prices: A theory of market equilibrium under conditions of risk', *Journal of Finance*, **19**(3), 425–42.

Sharpe, W.F. (1967), 'A simplified model of portfolio analysis', *Management Science*, **13**, 277–93.

Sheikh, A.Z. and H. Qiao (2009), *Non-normality of Market Returns: A Framework for Asset Allocation Decision-making*, New York: J.P. Morgan Asset Management.

Soros, G. (2009), *The Crash of 2008 and What It Means: The New Paradigm for Financial Markets*, New York: Perseus.

Working, H. (1956), 'New ideas and methods for price research', *Journal of Farm Economics*, **38**(5), 1427–36.

9. Teaching and learning with historical perspectives

Stephanie Fuller

1 INTRODUCTION

Teaching the history of economic thought is fast becoming an important topic of debate and discussion within economics teaching as the publication of this volume shows. But the use of historical perspectives in teaching is an issue of much wider relevance across higher education. The motivations and challenges behind implementing this kind of approach are specific to each discipline; however, there are things that we can learn from a range of subjects to help inform teaching the history of economic thought and teaching with historical perspectives more widely. This chapter explores the debates around teaching with historical perspectives in a range of subjects, focusing on some of the practical approaches used by teachers and exploring the impact of this pedagogical approach on students.[1]

One of the most important roles of historical perspectives in teaching is to offer new perspectives on modern issues or problems, and to challenge assumptions that students may bring to bear on courses. For example, taking a historical perspective on a media studies course, it can become clear that 'new media' is not a new phenomenon at all. The same concerns, alarms and shifts have happened over and over again, with the advent of books, newspapers, movies and television. Another key role of teaching with historical perspectives is as a form of induction into a discipline or profession. For medical education, some have argued that studying the evolution of medical science as a profession fosters a sense of belonging and solidarity of professionals, or 'nostalgic professionalism' (Bryan and Longo, 2013, p. 97). This idea is similar to that of induction into a 'community of practice' (Lave and Wenger, 1991, p. 63), a commonly advocated approach to enhancing student engagement. Similarly, for mathematics, teaching the history of the discipline is not always seen as being directly relevant to students studying the subject today. However, others argue that these historical perspectives are vitally important. Understanding the wider impact of a discipline beyond the immediate content being studied can be hugely important for subjects like maths, and helping students to see the connections between the subject matter and society is an important skill that they will likely need in future employment.

For humanities subjects it is much more common for students to be asked to consider historical contexts when studying a text, film, or artwork, and perhaps also to explore what, for example, literary critics writing at the time a novel was published thought about it. Skills in reading historically, establishing links and causation between events, and an understanding of the limitations in our understanding when looking at the past through sources and the lens of the present, are perhaps more readily integrated into many humanities subjects. These subjects are often already quite interdisciplinary in nature, and from the outset students are supported in developing these kinds of skills. However, there is still much room to enhance and build on this area.

In contrast, an economics student may be expecting their course to have a strong mathematical focus and to be asked to learn and apply formulas. Teachers can face a great challenge in supporting these students to develop skills in historical analysis if they want to ask them to consider historical theories or case studies as part of an economics degree. Communicating clearly to students the reasons why bringing a historical perspective to their studies is important is a large part of the issue. This is a matter of some debate in other disciplines as well; while some medical educators claim that learning about the history of medicine is irrelevant to today's trainee doctors, others argue that it is a vital part of developing the professionalism and wider skills that doctors will need in their careers.

Teaching with historical perspectives can play a crucial role in higher education because universities do not exist to simply deliver content to students, but also to induct them into disciplines and professions. Incorporating historical perspectives is also a powerful way of introducing interdisciplinary learning into a subject. Using this approach we can invite students to think historically about their subject in addition to learning the academic content of the course, helping students develop critical thinking, offering them different perspectives on issues, and better equipping them to tackle real-life problems that do not fall neatly into disciplinary areas.

2   CHALLENGING ASSUMPTIONS AND WIDER PERSPECTIVES

One of the most important roles of historical perspectives in teaching is to offer new perspectives on modern issues or problems, and to challenge assumptions that students may bring to bear on courses. On this aspect I will begin with some personal experience. While I am now working in educational development, my background is in English literature, cultural studies and media studies. I left school with a complete lack of interest in history and spent my degree and MA studying only the most recent texts and case studies that I could find. But it became apparent that engaging with historical ideas would be very important to succeeding in my degrees; when asked to grapple with concepts like postmodernism and poststructuralism, there is no way to begin to understand them except by investigating what went before – what are they 'post'? I wound up undertaking a historical study for my PhD and I found archival research and analysis of historical approaches to the issues I was researching the most rewarding and enlightening part of the project.

Historical perspectives were equally important when teaching media studies. Like me, my students were very keen to study all things new, and far less interested in anything historical. I found them very quick to support theories and approaches that understood the digital and the Internet as a complete break from what had gone before – the idea that new media changed everything including the ways we read and write, the way we comprehend, and our attention spans. However, taking a historical perspective, it is clear that 'new media' is not a new phenomenon at all, and the same concerns, alarms and shifts have happened over and over again, with the advent of books, newspapers, movies and television. Students were amazed to see that authors writing in the sixteenth and seventeenth centuries about books voiced many of the same concerns we might have about the Internet and digital age today. Erasmus (1466–1536) wrote of 'swarms of books ... [that are] ... foolish, ignorant, malignant, libellous, mad, impious and subversive'. While Descartes (1596–1650) extolled: 'even if all knowledge could be found in books, where it is mixed in with so many useless things and confusingly heaped in such large volumes, it would take longer to read those books than we have to live in this life and more effort to select the useful things than to find them oneself'. These voices from the sixteenth and seventeenth centuries question the overwhelming volume of books being published, and condemn the fact that many are ignorant or useless, and the time it takes to sift through the huge volumes of texts to find anything useful. These sentiments are likely very familiar to any regular user of the Internet today. Seen in this new historical context, students were able to understand that the Internet is just the latest in a very long line of new media.

However, many media studies degrees lack the historical perspective that would set today's social and digital media within an entirely new framework and give students an understanding of the way in which each 'new media' that has been developed (newspapers, books, television, film and the Internet) impacted upon and influenced its contemporary culture. With this understanding, we can begin to draw comparisons between our era and others, perhaps even learning useful lessons from the past; students have their assumptions about digital media and the Internet challenged. Historical perspectives are vitally important in humanities subjects like media and cultural studies for giving students broader perspectives, challenging assumptions, and helping them understand contemporary issues and theories that the disciplines are tackling.

For many humanities subjects, historical perspectives are already embedded within the subject matter. This can take a variety of forms. At a programme level, humanities students are more likely to be able to choose elective modules from a variety of courses that may include more traditionally historical modules run by a history department. Within many non-history degrees, students can also choose to take modules with a specific historical focus. For example, many literature modules are historical in nature as they often incorporate social, cultural and political contexts of texts into their remit. Other degrees are integrally historical in nature, such as art history or war studies.

As Julie Thompson Klein (2005) argues, despite the often restrictive disciplinary organization of university departments, most humanities subjects are interdisciplinary in nature and explore this aspect explicitly. The interdisciplinarity of today's humanities subjects is generally understood to be a result of a series of 'turns' in humanities thinking in the late twentieth century, such as poststructuralist, postmodern, feminist, African American, and geographic. These topics encouraged scholars in a wide variety of fields to tackle these broad ranging issues, bringing their own disciplinary knowledge in close contact with work being undertaken in cognate fields (Klein, 2005, pp. 53–4). However, the absence of many postdisciplinary structures within universities (such as cultural studies or critical studies departments) means that most interdisciplinary work still operates at the level of programmes, modules or individual topics within the humanities. In part because of this, it is useful to consider teaching with historical perspectives as a method of interdisciplinary learning and teaching, and to explore what existing interdisciplinary methods can offer those incorporating historical perspectives to their teaching.

A whole range of different teaching and learning activities have come to be labelled as interdisciplinary, from the opportunity for students to take a standalone module from another discipline, to co- or team-taught courses that bring together lecturers from different fields, to courses that centre fully around an interdisciplinary topic or issue. As Lyall et al. suggest in a report written for the Higher Education Academy, the broader term 'integrative learning' seems more appropriate for many of these activities, whereas '[t]ruly interdisciplinary models restructure the curriculum with explicitly integrative activities that are typically theme-based, problem-based, or question-based, and organised within a curriculum that has a spine of required core courses ensuring attention is paid to interdisciplinary theory, concepts and methods' (Lyall et al., 2015, p. v; see also Klein, 2005).

Just as there are a wide range of manifestations of interdisciplinary teaching and learning, there is equally as broad a range of motives for introducing interdisciplinarity in higher education. Interdisciplinary approaches are widely recognized as becoming more and more necessary to tackle the complex global challenges of today's world. The broader range of skills and knowledge offered to students may also help boost their employment chances, a vital aspect of the debate that will be discussed in more detail below. However, the opportunity to take a new perspective on issues or to explore a range of different viewpoints and critical perspectives is one of the most important, and sometimes overlooked, benefits of interdisciplinary education. Interdisciplinary programme directors identify some of the key skills that students develop on their courses as the 'ability to synthesise', 'appreciation of diverse perspectives' and 'flexible, critical thinking' (Lyall et al., 2015, p. 36). Teaching with historical perspectives can be an important way of helping to develop these skills in students.

Programme-level interdisciplinary initiatives are being introduced at universities around the world, with the University of Melbourne's 'Melbourne Curriculum' (initially called the 'Melbourne Model') leading the way as one of the first of these institution-led interdisciplinary initiatives. This curriculum model was introduced in 2008 with the aim of producing graduates with breadth as well as depth. The university's website claims that the model improves critical engagement, research capacity and peer interaction. Universities around the world have since followed suit, with two notable UK examples being the University of Aberdeen's Enhanced Study Options and the University of Manchester's University College for Interdisciplinary Learning (UCOL). At Manchester, UCOL seeks to 'broaden students' minds, encourage curiosity and enhance their employability', with the ultimate aim of students accessing at least 30 credits of UCOL courses throughout their degree.

The debate around interdisciplinary teaching and learning is highly relevant to this discussion of teaching with historical perspectives. Whether it is vital to discriminate between 'truly' interdisciplinary models and approaches that are merely 'multidisciplinary' or 'transdisciplinary' is a wider question outside the scope of this chapter. However, the introduction of historical perspectives to teaching enables lecturers to shift programmes, modules or even individual topics towards a more interdisciplinary experience for students, giving them many of the benefits such as a wider range of skills, better employment prospects as well as enhanced critical engagement and wider perspectives.

There are, of course, challenges in implementing this kind of approach. At a programme level, while the option to study modules from different schools or faculties, or modules about the history of a discipline is of benefit to students, time also needs to be built into programmes to help students integrate these different experiences and to bring the differing elements of their degree together to some extent. This is in order to help them make sense of their interdisciplinary learning experience. At a modular level, students could be offered the chance to study wide-ranging modules that are theme, problem or question based and seek to empower students to explore interdisciplinary methods and approaches. At the level of a single topic or lecture, simply introducing students to the historical, cultural and social contexts of the topic, theory or approach being studied can be a way of integrating an interdisciplinary perspective. This may require the development of new teaching methods, but Lyall et al.'s report (2015, p. 36) outlines a range of approaches that are currently in use across the sector to help enable interdisciplinary learning and teaching which may provide some useful starting points:

- Co-teaching – with lecturers from different subject areas, members of industry, or co-creation of course syllabus or content. Bringing in a lecturer who can place the topic in historical, cultural or social contexts, or provide a different perspective on materials.
- Project-based learning or case study methods – this can get students involved in researching around a topic, including its historical contexts and the historical situation from which it emerged and exploring cases from a range of different perspectives.
- Innovative teaching methods – 'flipped learning' where students spend classroom time on activities and direct instruction takes place in their own time, and 'learning to learn' where students reflect on the learning experience.
- Peer assessment and/or peer-assisted learning – students bring different knowledge and disciplinary expertise to bear on their university learning and so this can be a valuable student-led interdisciplinary approach.

3   INDUCTION INTO A DISCIPLINE/ PROFESSION

Many other subjects studied by students at university have a far more vocational focus, medicine being one of the clearest examples. There is a great deal of debate around the inclusion of medical history within medical education; some authors argue that it detracts from the more critical study of contemporary medical practice, while its proponents attest that it plays a key role in acting as a form of induction into the profession. The study of medical history has developed into an independent interdisciplinary field, while many medical degrees now offer students an elective module in the history of medicine.[2]

Highlighting the importance of studying the evolution of medical science as a profession, Bryan and Longo (2013) claim that it fosters a sense of belonging and solidarity of professionals, enabling students to develop a 'nostalgic professionalism'. In an era when the higher education and healthcare sectors are under threats from the encroachment of capitalism and government regulation, these authors see a focus on medicine as a profession rather than a trade as a way of encouraging students to become activists with a sense of 'civic responsibility' (p. 97). Similarly, Shedlock, Sims and Kubilius (2012) found that studying medical history was important to students because of 'what it teaches them about the medical profession and how it has developed over time' (p. 140). However, other scholars have argued that there is little point in teaching humanities or medical history to medical students because medicine is becoming a more dehumanized and technical profession (e.g., Gourevitch, 1999; Swick and Simpson, 1998).

Bryan and Longo provide a useful list of the ways in which the history of medicine can benefit medical students, which I believe can be applied to other disciplinary contexts. For example, they suggest medical history can 'impart a sense of continuity with the past' and introduce the notion of 'the limitations of our knowledge at any given time' (2013, p. 99). These are useful ideas for students of many disciplines to engage with, whether they are part of a vocational course or a more disciplinary-based programme. Equally, some of the methodologies Bryan and Longo present can be highly relevant for teachers of other subjects, such as identifying a faculty lead for promoting the history of a discipline, drawing on retired colleagues and those from other disciplines for input into teaching, or incorporating historical perspectives into mentoring, research projects or promoting special interest groups on the topic among students (p. 100). Ideas for ways of incorporating historical perspectives into research projects or case-based learning could include asking students to explore the lives of key historical figures in a discipline or examining key moments in the development of disciplinary techniques and theories.

Bryan and Longo's idea of 'nostalgic professionalism' is similar to that of induction into a 'community of practice' (Lave and Wenger, 1991), a commonly advocated approach to enhancing student engagement. With this approach, students are incorporated into an active professional network while they are still learning, and encouraged to take part, enabling them to identify with the professionals and helping them to engage in active, participatory learning. As a social constructivist attitude to learning, Lave and Wenger's approach emphasizes the need for learning to be personal and social, and for the line between student and professional to be broken down. The history of medicine can therefore provide an opportunity to 'humanize' the subject matter by introducing the people behind scientific achievements. Students may also be encouraged to think of themselves as part of this group of doctors, becoming part of the community of practice and helping to understand their training as a continuous element of their professional careers.

A community of practice may be a useful way to access historical perspectives in other disciplines too. Providing students with spaces to create their own communities and to interact with professional communities (described as 'legitimate peripheral participation' by Lave and Wenger) can offer opportunities to find out about the history of a profession or discipline. Lave and Wenger describe legitimate peripheral participation as a way of theorizing learning as apprenticeship; 'a process of becoming a member of a sustained community of practice. Developing an identity as a member of a community and becoming knowledgably skilful are part of the same process, with the former motivating, shaping, and giving meaning to the latter, which it subsumes' (Lave and Wenger, 1991, p. 65). Learning about and identifying with previous practitioners of their discipline can be an effective way of enhancing student learning, development and engagement.

The kind of civic responsibility that Bryan and Longo write about engendering through nostalgic professionalism may also be important for other disciplines. Non-vocational disciplines such as the humanities are feeling under increased threat from market and capitalist forces in higher education (Lynch, 2006). Engaging with the critical concepts of disciplinarity and interdisciplinarity, what marks the boundaries and borderlines of subject areas, and the history of a discipline and its thinkers can be a useful way of encouraging students to challenge those who would question the value of these subjects in higher education.

There are also skills that we may want students to leave higher education with that go beyond the content of a course, even a vocational programme such as medicine. The community of practice approach can help build these, and help students understand the value of these wider skills. Shedlock et al. (2012) argue that the history of medicine encourages lifelong learning and develops skills in research and independent learning that students will need when they are doctors, as they will be expected to be able to keep up to date with new developments in their area of expertise. In addition to the ideas of professionalism and induction into a professional community, the inclusion of medical history within a medical degree clearly offers students a broader range of skills. Further, an HEA workshop on teaching the history of medicine concluded that it can help boost empathy with patients and improve skills in handling scientific information (Long, 2008). Studying the history of medicine therefore operates much like the opportunity to study optional modules from different disciplines, by enabling students to learn and use a different range of skills and expertise than those offered within their core degree subject, and by exploring the connections between these different disciplines and skills. Universities across the world have been formalizing these wider skills into statements of attributes that their graduates are expected to gain during their programmes; I will consider graduate attributes in more detail below.

4   SEEING BEYOND THE DISCIPLINE

As for medicine, in mathematics, teaching the history of the discipline is not always understood as something that is directly relevant to students studying the subject today. For example, Michael Fried contends that 'the commitment to teach the modern mathematics and modern mathematical techniques necessary in the pure and applied sciences forces one either to trivialize history or to distort it' (2001, p. 391). However, others contend that studying the history of mathematics can have huge benefits for students' disciplinary skills. Weng Kin Ho argues that using the history of mathematics has wide-ranging benefits for students' maths education itself: '(1) increasing the students' motivation and develop a positive attitude towards mathematics; (2) helping explain difficulties and confusion that students encounter via an analysis of the development of mathematics; (3) enhancing the development of students' mathematical reasoning skills by the use of historical problems; and (4) revealing the humanistic aspects of mathematical knowledge' (2008, pp. 2–3).

Historical perspectives on mathematics are also seen as important for other reasons beyond immediate disciplinary skills. Wilson and Chauvot (2000, p. 642) contend that it 'sharpens problem-solving skills, lays a foundation for better understanding, helps students make mathematical connections, and highlights the interaction between mathematics and society'. Understanding the relationship between the subject matter and wider society can be of particular benefit to students of disciplines such as maths. Typically, maths students will not have the opportunity to take modules from other disciplines during their degrees, and so the inclusion of an option on the history of the subject offers students the benefits of a taste of interdisciplinary education.

Helping maths students to see the connections between their subject matter and society is an important skill that they will likely need in future employment. Arguing this passionately, Jim Bidwell writes that through historical perspectives 'we can rescue students from the island of mathematics and relocate them on the mainland of life that contains mathematics that is open, alive, full of emotion, and always interesting' (1993, p. 461). Bidwell highlights the importance of exploring the connections between maths and the wider world that students will put into practice when they enter the world of work.

Here again, the benefits of teaching with historical perspectives are articulated in interdisciplinary terms through more explicitly bringing to the fore the subject's connections to the wider world. This idea is also connected to the idea of 'graduate attributes' and the wider skills that universities aim to develop in their students. Graduate skills are a key issue for universities today, with almost all UK universities now possessing a statement of graduate attributes that sets out the range of skills that their students should expect to achieve while studying with them. Bowden et al. (2002) define graduate attributes as:

> [. . .]the qualities, skills and understandings a university community agrees its students should develop during their time with the institution. These attributes include but go beyond the disciplinary expertise or technical knowledge that has traditionally formed the core of most university courses. They are qualities that also prepare graduates as agents of social good in an unknown future.

This definition highlights the need for students' development to go beyond 'disciplinary expertise' in order to prepare graduates for their future, and to engender a sense of responsibility, or 'social good'. Similarly, Simon Barrie (2004) describes graduate attributes as 'the skills, knowledge and abilities of university graduates, beyond disciplinary content knowledge, which are applicable to a range of contexts' (p. 262).

Programmes and modules that incorporate historical perspectives can clearly be harnessed as part of the drive towards developing graduate attributes in students. Resistance to the inclusion of this approach may also be linked to resistance to the idea of graduate attributes. This issue always provokes a great deal of debate when I have addressed it in seminars with new academic staff at my institution. Many lecturers support the development of wider skills in students as a force for good that broadens their horizons, develops critical thinking and enhances their job prospects. However, others question whether there is space within the curriculum in some disciplines for this kind of activity. For instance, some lecturers argue that their curricula are already stretched to the extreme and question how programme teams could condense this further or cope with losing time for content delivery in order to provide space for additional activities for students.

These lecturers also questioned whether the university's aim was to create students who were good at their discipline, or graduates of an entirely commercialized process aimed solely at ticking the degree box and getting them a job.[3] While I agree there is a real concern about the links between schemes such as graduate attributes and the marketization of higher education, this view often belies the very real employment needs of students. Many students do not have the connections or social capital to take them directly into graduate-level jobs, and the opportunities provided through graduate attributes initiatives to develop a wider set of skills and qualities are vital (Tomlinson, 2008). Universities' emphasis on moral and social responsibility in their graduate attribute statements goes some way to identifying and addressing this issue.[4]

I believe that developing teaching using historical perspectives on a discipline can address many of the questions within this wider debate around graduate attributes. It offers students an opportunity to enhance disciplinary skills and expertise alongside the benefits of interdisciplinary education and the development of wider skills and attributes. It can fit into the curriculum in a wide variety of ways and provides a link between disciplines and the wider world that, whatever our view on the purpose of higher education, is undeniably something that students will need to be able to do once they graduate.

5 CONCLUSION

Incorporating historical perspectives is a powerful way of introducing interdisciplinary learning into a subject by inviting students to think historically about their subject in addition to learning the academic content of the course. Some of the key motivations behind the development of interdisciplinary teaching and learning models are to help students develop critical thinking, offer them different perspectives on issues, and to better equip them to tackle real-life problems that do not fall neatly into disciplinary areas. Thinking about teaching with historical perspectives as a form of interdisciplinary teaching might be a useful way of further exploring this area of work, and of developing effective methods and means of supporting students in this kind of learning.

Fink (2003) argues that interdisciplinary teaching promotes 'significant learning'; meaningful, lasting learning experiences that constitute a deep learning experience for students. Fink has identified six elements of the educational process that are useful to consider when thinking about introducing interdisciplinary teaching and learning. These can also serve as practical pointers for developing historical perspectives in teaching:

- foundational knowledge – acquiring information and understanding ideas;
- application – acquiring an understanding of how and when to use skills;
- integration – the capacity to connect ideas;
- human dimension – recognition of the social and personal implications of issues;
- caring – acknowledgement of the role of feelings, interests, and values;
- learning how-to-learn – obtaining insights into the process of learning (Fink, 2003, p. 35).

Several of these aspects are particularly relevant strategies for teaching with historical perspectives. The need to provide students with foundational knowledge is crucial when thinking about origins of disciplines and ideas. Helping students to understand these first, before tackling the most recent or cutting-edge work can be a useful teaching strategy. An appreciation of the real-life applications of work is vitally important for motivating students and helping them see beyond the discipline and academic content itself; historical examples and case studies are a great way of bringing this into teaching. Further, teaching with historical perspectives is a method for integrating ideas and topics, and can be achieved by inviting students to connect different concepts, approaches and theories from different historical periods and to compare or contrast them. Historical perspectives also enable students to explore the human dimension of an issue; what the broader social implications are, how the subject matter relates to the real world, how has this changed over time, and how it has impacted on people and society in different periods.

Teaching with historical perspectives is crucial in higher education because we are not just here to deliver content to students, but also to induct them into disciplines and professions. Understanding the history of a discipline plays an important role in this. It is not just the subject matter at hand that we want students to go away with an understanding of, but also a much wider sense of the broader debates within a discipline, where the discipline's boundaries lie and overlap, and where and how it interacts with society and the wider world. The question of teaching with historical perspectives is also connected to some of the most fundamental debates around the purpose of higher education: whether higher education is limited only to delivering disciplinary content and academic knowledge, or whether its purpose is to develop broader graduate and employability skills in students. Historical perspectives on a discipline, its development, key figures or ideas can be a way of coupling the enhancement of disciplinary skills with the development of wider skills and perspectives and beginning to bridge the two sides of this debate.

NOTES

1. A discussion of what constitutes 'history' and the practices and boundaries of this discipline is outside of the scope of this chapter. I use the term 'historical perspectives' to indicate any form of engagement with the history of a subject area, historical sources or historical contexts that educators may incorporate into

their teaching. For detailed discussions of history and its study see, for example, McRaild and Black (2007) and Fea (2013).

2. While I do not focus on interdisciplinarity in medical education, it is interesting to note that multidisciplinary education and learning is an important emphasis in many medical degrees, with the idea that the different healthcare professions can learn a great deal from interacting with each other, and that multidisciplinary teams are the best approach to treating patients.

3. This issue is explored in, for example, Molesworth, Scullion and Nixon (2011) and Green, Hammer and Star (2009).

4. See, for example, the Queen Mary University of London Statement of Graduate Attributes, which includes the attribute 'accept the responsibilities that come from taking a global perspective', accessed 19 December 2017 at http://www.qmul.ac.uk/docs/gacep/38598.pdf.

REFERENCES

Barrie, S. (2004), 'A research-based approach to generic graduate attributes policy', *Higher Education Research & Development*, **23**(3), 261–75.

Bidwell, J. (1993), 'Humanize your classroom with the history of mathematics', *The Mathematics Teacher*, **86**(6), 461–4.

Bowden, J., G. Hart, B. King, K. Trigwell and O. Watts (2002), 'Generic capabilities of ATN university graduates', accessed 19 December 2017 at http://www.scirp.org/(S(lz5mqp453edsnp55rrgjct55))/reference/ReferencesPapers.aspx?ReferenceID=870920.

Bryan, C. and L.D. Longo (2013), 'Perspective: Teaching and mentoring the history of medicine: An Oslerian perspective', *Academic Medicine*, **88**(1), 97–101.

Fea, J. (2013), *Why Study History: Reflecting on the Importance of the Past*, Grand Rapids, MI: Baker Academic.

Fink, L.D. (2003), *Creating Significant Learning Experiences: An Integrated Approach to Designing College Courses*, accessed 21 December 2017 at https://www.unl.edu/philosophy/%5BL._Dee_Fink%5D_Creating_Significant_Learning_Experi(BookZZ.org).pdf.

Fried, M. (2001), 'Can mathematics education and history of mathematics coexist?', *Science & Education*, **10**(4), 391–408.

Gourevitch, D. (1999), 'The history of medical teaching', *Lancet*, **2000**(354), 33.

Green, W., S. Hammer and C. Star (2009), 'Facing up to the challenge: Why develop graduate attributes?', *Higher Education Research and Development*, **28**(1), 17–29.

Ho, W.K. (2008), 'Using history of mathematics in the teaching and learning of mathematics in Singapore', in *Proceedings of 1st Raffles International Conference on Education*, 1–38, Singapore.

Klein, J.T. (2005), *Humanities, Culture and Interdisciplinarity: The Changing American Academy*, Albany, NY: State University of New York Press.

Lave, J. and E. Wenger (1991), *Situated Learning: Legitimate Peripheral Participation*, Cambridge, UK: Cambridge University Press.

Long, V. (2008), 'Teaching medical history', UK Higher Education Academy, accessed 13 February 2017 at https://www.heacademy.ac.uk/resource/teaching-medical-history.

Lyall, C., L. Meagher, J. Bandola and A. Kettle (2015), *Interdisciplinary Provision in Higher Education: Current and Future Challenges*, UK Higher Education Academy, accessed 13 February 2017 at https://www.heacademy.ac.uk/sites/default/files/interdisciplinary_provision_in_he.pdf.

Lynch, K. (2006), 'Neo-liberalism and marketisation: The implications for higher education', *European Educational Research Journal*, 5(1), 1–17.

McRaild, D. and J. Black (2007), *Studying History*, Basingstoke: Palgrave Macmillan.

Molesworth, M., R. Scullion and E. Nixon (2011), *The Marketisation of Higher Education and the Student as Consumer*, London and New York: Routledge.

Shedlock, J., R.H. Sims and R.K. Kubilius (2012), 'Promoting and teaching the history of medicine in a medical school curriculum', *Journal of the Medical Library Association*, 100(2), 138–41.

Swick, H.M. and D.E. Simpson (1998), 'Another professional-skills course worth nothing', *Academic Medicine*, 73(7), 725.

Tomlinson, M. (2008), '"The degree is not enough": Students' perceptions of the role of higher education credentials for graduate work and employability', *British Journal of Sociology of Education*, 29(1), 49–61.

University of Aberdeen, 'Enhanced Study Options', accessed 19 December 2017 at https://www.abdn.ac.uk/study/undergraduate/enhanced-study-options-1518.php.

University of Manchester, 'University College for Interdisciplinary Learning', accessed 13 February 2017 at http://www.college.manchester.ac.uk/.

University of Melbourne, 'The Melbourne Curriculum', accessed 13 February 2017 at http://provost.unimelb.edu.au/teaching-learning/melbourne-curriculum; Undergraduate course directory: https://course-search.unimelb.edu.au/undergrad.

Wilson, P.S. and J.B. Chauvot (2000), 'Who? How? What? A strategy for using history to teach mathematics', *The Mathematics Teacher*, 93(8), 642–45.

Index